Jean Baudrillard: From Hyperreality to Disappearance

Jean Baudrillard: From Hyperreality to Disappearance

Uncollected Interviews

Edited by Richard G. Smith and
David B. Clarke

EDINBURGH
University Press

Edinburgh University Press Ltd
The Tun – Holyrood Road
12(2f) Jackson's Entry
Edinburgh EH8 8PJ
www.euppublishing.com

Typeset in 10.5/13 pt Sabon by
Servis Filmsetting Ltd, Stockport, Cheshire,
and printed and bound in Great Britain by
CPI Group (UK) Ltd, Croydon CR0 4YY

A CIP record for this book is available from the British Library

ISBN 978 0 7486 9428 0 (hardback)
ISBN 978 0 7486 9430 3 (webready PDF)
ISBN 978 0 7486 9429 7 (paperback)
ISBN 978 0 7486 9431 0 (epub)

Published with the support of the Edinburgh University Scholarly Publishing Initiatives Fund.

Contents

Acknowledgements

We thank all those who have kindly granted their permission for us to reproduce copyrighted material. Full credit is provided to copyright holders following each interview. While considerable effort has been made to trace and contact copyright holders prior to publication, the editors and publishers apologise for any oversights or omissions, and if notified will endeavour to remedy these at the earliest opportunity. We would particularly like to thank Chris Turner and Carol Macdonald for their support in preparing this book.

Introduction: Not Forgetting Baudrillard

> [T]hey don't like what I have to say, but they come to me anyway, because they need someone to say something different, the opposite of everyone else.
>
> Jean Baudrillard (in Hegarty 2004: 134)

> Most of the time people want a facsimile . . . You feel like a hostage, you feel as if you've been taken hostage.
>
> Jean Baudrillard (in Gane 1993: 199)

Disappearances, like appearances, can be deceptive. Since his untimely death on 6 March 2007, at the age of 77, Jean Baudrillard's work has, perhaps inevitably, slipped from the kind of mainstream prominence that once routinely drew not only academics but also artists and journalists into its orbit. At the same time, Baudrillard's work – by turns prescient, perceptive, provocative and profound – has continued to grow in stature and attract new interest.[1] One of the great thinkers of disappearance, Baudrillard astutely grasped its vicissitudes and anticipated its effects. 'Disappearing is of a far higher order of necessity' than death, he wrote: 'You must not leave it to biology to decide when you will disappear. To disappear is to pass into an enigmatic state which is neither life nor death' (1990: 24). In contradistinction to the finality of death, disappearance is not an irreversible event: 'What has disappeared has every chance of reappearing' (Baudrillard 1990: 92). There is, then, beyond biology, an aesthetics of disappearance, an art of disappearance that many fail to master, neglecting to withdraw from the world before the point at which they have nothing left to say. Baudrillard, in contrast, was a grand master of the art of disappearance.

Over the course of his career, from a relatively early point in fact, Baudrillard came to eschew the trappings of conventional academic engagement, eventually to emerge as a commentator capable of wearing lightly the most pressing of concerns, extracting hidden truths directly from the surface of contemporary events, and taking a distinct pleasure in nudging towards their furtive destiny things that were only too ready to fall. Far from casually courting controversy, as some critics sought to impute, Baudrillard's sometimes audacious reasoning followed an impeccable logic. Rather than an obscene will to provoke, Baudrillard's occasionally wilful provocations refined and rehearsed a sophisticated theory of an obscene world. Understandably, Baudrillard felt under no obligation to dilute his insights, following (and often anticipating) events with an unflinching compulsion to tell it like it is. This is as evident in the growing number of interviews that accompanied his rising fame as it is in his writings.

While Baudrillard resolutely refused to be pressed into explaining himself – still less into justifying his position – in the many interviews he granted, he frequently took significant pains to elucidate and explicate his ideas. Typically engaging his interlocutors somewhat uncomfortably, he was nonetheless adroit at correcting misapprehensions, discriminating his own line of thought from that of others, or simply clarifying, restating and affirming his own position. It is in this respect that this volume of interviews is of particular value – gathering together a wide range of often forgotten or otherwise hard-to-find interviews spanning the key decades of Baudrillard's career. Like Gane's seminal *Baudrillard Live* (1993), the present collection permits an alternative route into Baudrillard's thought, operating on a different register to his writings without sacrificing or departing from their rigour – at least when a certain level of intensity is attained. Baudrillard typically cared less about convincing others than he did about expressing his understanding with absolute conviction. In this respect, interviews can reach an intensity that lends them a crucial role, despite (or even because of) the attendant risks they carry. Responding to Gane's (1993: 199) question on the nature of the interview, Baudrillard describes it as 'an adventure – but a problematic one'. Interviews can be unpredictable, hijacked for particular purposes by sometimes ill-informed interviewers, and, worst of all, reduced to a mere matter of communication: the banal exchange of information. The risks for the reader extend to Baudrillard's own apparent disregard for the interview format: by all accounts he rarely saw fit to involve himself in follow-up corrections or amendments, or otherwise engage with the resulting text once he had walked away from an interview. Yet the fact that something is always at stake in the interview situation necessarily entails, as Genosko (1998: 18) notes, that the interview 'belongs to the universe of seduction, whose terms are those of play, challenge, reversibility, and the duel'. The interview's agonistic logic resonates with the most vital elements of Baudrillard's conceptual universe.

For those unfamiliar with Baudrillard's work, it is worth simply stating that it traced an ever more refined, yet consistently radical diagnosis of the contemporary condition. Beginning with an oblique take on the triangulation of Marx, Freud and Saussure that sustained structuralism, Baudrillard discerned the unacknowledged complicity of critical thought with its supposed target. If Marx sailed too close to the principle of production on which capitalism was based to escape its purview; if Freud found himself seduced by the mirror of desire; and if Saussure's account of meaning resonated all too clearly with the principle of equivalence governing commodity exchange, Baudrillard found a higher logic at work in so-called primitive societies: the logic of the challenge, the raising of the stakes defining symbolic exchange. Drawing on the logic of the gift unearthed by Mauss and pressed to the limit in Bataille's principle of expenditure, and counterposing the Saussure of the *Anagrams* to the *Course in General Linguistics*, Baudrillard disclosed a profound sense in which modernity disavowed certain fundamental principles that it singularly failed to escape. In societies uncontaminated by modernity – societies unbeholden to the reality principle and heedless of the law of value – the principle of ambivalence held sway. This principle has, in fact, remained intact, Baudrillard maintained, despite (or perhaps even because of) modernity's sustained efforts to annihilate ambivalence by means of equivalence. It was this basic insight that set the course of Baudrillard's subsequent trajectory.

Baudrillard's work proceeded to develop via a dazzling series of conceptions which nonetheless retained a remarkable consistency – refining and extending his fundamental insight through an intensely creative set of formulations, offering consistently fresh perspectives from a range of novel vantage points. Thus, Baudrillard traced the destiny of the modern world in accordance with the principle of seduction rather than production. He explored the way in which reality progressively betrayed its own principle, ushering in a hyperreal world of simulacra and simulation. Switching allegiances from critical theory to fatal theory, he increasingly adopted the vantage point of the object rather than that of the subject. He highlighted the implosion of reality and illusion; the involution of Good and Evil; the short-circuiting of truth and falsity; the reversibility of appearance and disappearance; and so on. While these very terms might seem like so many unfortunate binary oppositions, Baudrillard's point is precisely that they appear as such from one direction only: from the perspective that modernity tried to instate. Yet in attempting to dissent from a higher order of logic, that logic was destined to wreak its revenge. For example, while the reality principle thrives on the opposition it posits between the real and the imaginary, the symbolic knows nothing of such oppositions. In attempting to subjugate the world to the reality principle, modernity was destined not to rid the world of illusion but to bring about the radical disillusion of the world. Likewise with Good and Evil:

> Only Good posits itself as such; Evil does not posit itself at all. Like the Nothing, of which it is the analogon, it is perfect because it is opposed to nothing. Good and Evil, like masculine and feminine, are asymmetric: they are not the mirrors, nor the complements, nor the opposites of each other. The relation between them might, rather, be described as ironic. One of the terms scoffs at the other and at its own positing. (Baudrillard 2001: 96)

The irony is palpable in the 'irresistible tendency of Good to produce negative counter-effects', which is 'equalled only by the secret inclination of Evil ultimately to produce Good' (Baudrillard 2001: 96). Such insights, rendered supremely visible by Baudrillard's unique perspective, are scattered throughout the interviews assembled here.

It remains to say a little more of the interviews comprising the body of this text. The majority of these interviews have previously appeared elsewhere in English or English-language translation (typically from the French, German, or in one case Norwegian), with the exception of the first. Originally published in French in 1990, the opening interview has been translated especially for the present volume by Chris Turner. Despite departing from the chronological sequence otherwise governing the order of presentation – the remainder of the interviews follow the chronological sequence of their appearance in English – this interview serves as a kind of prelude, offering a valuable orientation to the genesis of Baudrillard's thought prior to the period from which the bulk of the interviews derive, in addition to developing a number of important themes in its own right. Given the date of Gane's *Baudrillard Live* (1993), the majority of the coverage of the present volume comprises more recent interviews. The two volumes do, however, overlap in terms of their chronology. Although they were not included in Gane's (1993) collection,[2] Interviews 1 to 8 were first published in English between 1986 and 1993. Interviews 9 to 23, by contrast, saw their publication in English between 1995 and 2011.[3] Originally appearing in a diverse range of publications – from academic books and journals to popular magazines and websites – the content of these interviews ranges over terrain as diverse as that covered in Baudrillard's writings: art, war, fashion, technology, globalisation, terrorism, politics, photography, pataphysics, simulation, America, hyperreality, disappearance, the fate of humanity, and so on. As ever, the tensions and contradictions of the interview form alluded to above are very much in evidence but, by the same token, remain as instructive as ever. The interminable game of appearances and disappearances is in play.

In line with the last point, it is fitting to close these prefatory remarks with a pair of quotations taken from, respectively, Gane's (1993) collection of interviews and the present volume, which might serve to sum up the relationship between the interviews Baudrillard gave and his writings. In the first, taken from Baudrillard's conversation with Gane (1993: 201), Baudrillard commented on the contradiction of involving himself in interviews at all:

> [S]trictly speaking, it's true that having made a critique of this form of communication which is vaguely humanist, vaguely dialogic, I should refuse to do that kind of thing ... But, then, one cannot but enter into the game. Even then, there is still something human in this to the extent that there is some kind of challenge in it, an altercation, perhaps. You have to defend yourself.

And from this volume:

> I think writing's already a way of concealing your voice, of getting back to a sort of secrecy. Some people produce visibility, others secrecy. My writing's more in the vein of recreating secrecy ... Logically, if there were a fulfilment of desire, that would be it. After withdrawing concepts from thought and words from the language, it follows logically that you should also withdraw yourself from the game, should let the 'I' not wreck the game but withdraw from it as an invisible actor – to merge with the rules of the game almost. (Interview 1)

To master the art of disappearance, Baudrillard sometimes showed himself, sometimes sought a certain invisibility. The results of this game of appearances and disappearances replicate its logic in the pages that follow.

NOTES ON ORGANISATION

There are four main points to note. First, unless otherwise indicated, the interviewer(s) for each interview also translated the interview into English. Secondly, any accompanying notes other than those deriving from the original are attributed to the editors. Thirdly, certain emendations have been made to conform to the Edinburgh University Press house style. Finally, we have given titles to interviews that lacked them originally.

NOTES

1. For example, in China – see Lu (2014), Yibing (2014), Yun (2014), Zhisheng (2011). In 2012, exhibitions of photographs by Baudrillard were held across China – at Times Museum of Canton, CAFA Art Museum and Tap Seac Gallery – and an international seminar dedicated to Baudrillard's work was held at Nanjing University.
2. None of the interviews in this collection were published in Gane (1993). Two of the interviews collected here do also appear, but with different titles, in J. Baudrillard (2005), *The Conspiracy of Art*, New York: Semiotext(e).
3. Interview 11 was first published in German in 1987 and first appeared in English in 1995.

REFERENCES

Baudrillard, J. (1990), *Cool Memories*, London: Verso.
Baudrillard, J. (2001), *Impossible Exchange*, London: Verso.
Gane, M. (ed.) (1993), *Baudrillard Live: Selected Interviews*, London: Routledge.
Genosko, G. (1998), *Undisciplined Theory*, London: Sage.
Hegarty, P. (2004), *Jean Baudrillard: Live Theory*, London: Continuum.
Lu, Y. (2014), 'French Theory in China', *Contemporary French and Francophone Studies* 18(1), 69–74.
Yibing, Z. (2014), *A Marxist Reading of Young Baudrillard: Throughout his Ordered Masks*, Istanbul: Canut International Publishers.
Yun, P. (2014), *Jean Baudrillard's Theory and its Spread in China*, Guangzhou: Jinan University Press.
Zhisheng, Z. (2011), *A Review on Marxist and Left Debates*, Berlin: Canut International Publishers.

1 Too Bad about Patagonia

Interview with Michel Jourde (MJ) and Hadrien Laroche (HL)

MJ/HL *Do you still chide yourself for your lack of an aura?*

I'm not the pope! . . . This is all down to my peasant heredity. Culture's always been something alien to me, something I've never been able to take. So I've always had a sense of being a bit coarse and vulgar. There's a laziness and off-handedness towards himself about the peasant – and morbid anxiety towards things. And a contempt for work – even if he works a lot. The peasant has neither aura nor destiny. That way, he's like an object. I feel something verging on indignation towards everything that assumes the overt – social or real – form of intelligence, culture and comfort. That's a thing I've never been able to get over. I couldn't even get through the first year of preparatory classes for the *grandes écoles*. I dropped out after three months. Once you get three intellectuals together, it's more than I can bear.

THE TRANSPARENCY OF EVIL: A LOW-RENT APOCALYPSE

MJ/HL *Three things are said about you. The first is that everybody's 'doing a Baudrillard' these days. For example, the evening news on TV where they're always talking about the disappearance of political power.*

I hadn't heard that one. That either means that what I'm saying shows my finger's on the pulse, though that's pretentious, extremely banal too, and not very flattering. Or else we're talking about an automatic product of television, of the way that particular machinery operates – redundancy. I hear it as a parody of what I might say. But you can't escape parody. What's the relationship between a raw, primary discourse and an analytic, theoretical one? There is a relationship, but it's neither direct nor automatic. When someone says 'They're doing a

Baudrillard', I don't believe it at all. And I don't want to believe it either [*laughter*] . . . because if that's how it is, it'd be better to stop right away.

MJ/HL *It's also said that Baudrillard is dated, since the eighties mark a return to moral values and 'agency'.*

Here I'd say we're talking about something that isn't just outdated, but hyper-outdated. This retro-valorisation, this rehabilitation of values is one more step towards the civilisation of emptiness. Saturation's an even better way of putting it. It's also been said that I was an 'eighties thinker'. As for 'postmodern', I've had my fill of that all over the world. People stick labels like that on you and you can't get free of them. What I did before *Symbolic Exchange and Death* (1976) belongs, admittedly, to another period. It's not the same kind of writing. There are things in there that were part of the particular zeitgeist, things from the disciplines of the day – semiology or psychoanalysis. It was around that time things changed for me.

MJ/HL *Last of all, when* The Transparency of Evil *came out (1990), it was said that Baudrillard represented a striking return to nineteenth-century reactionary thinking, to Joseph de Maistre and the battle against the Enlightenment, with its denial of the existence of evil . . .*

These are defensive over-interpretations. I don't feel that I've become reactionary. I feel I've just gone through my own ceiling – the ceiling I set myself in my writing – a bit earlier than I might otherwise have done. Apparently, as soon as you make some sort of leap, people are a bit disconcerted and, being unable to say anything about the work, they go in for projection. They speak of ideas as depressive, for example, because the ideas make *them* depressed. This happens automatically, with every leap forward – the first with *On Seduction* (1979), when I alienated almost everybody, and the second with *America* (1986) and *Cool Memories 1980–85*, when the change in the writing was more disconcerting. Since I'm less and less in step with the ideology of the times, the only thing they can do with me is consign me to an earlier age. Let me add that I'm now being seen as a nothingness-merchant, as the gravedigger of the apocalypse. This is as bad as it gets. And everyone's fallen in with that version of the low-rent apocalypse and there's nothing more to be done. Once they've arrived at that point, there's no one left to see things differently [*resigned smile*] . . . no one to read the book. But it's no use crying over it. That's the game. And in a way it confirms my analysis of the processes of defensive simulation, the aim of which is to neutralise. But that's to have things too conveniently my own way.

MJ/HL *In* Cool Memories 1980–85, *you criticise the kind of adulteration that you say Foucault was part of, producing a sort of rock and roll-style mania . . .*

Do I use that term?

MJ/HL *You write that the intellectual world 'is not very different from the popular world of rock music'.*[1]

That's hard on rock music [*laughter*] . . .

MJ/HL *And yet you appeared on the cover of* The Face?

I don't want to add another mechanism of denial that would make everything even more complicated. It's not that thought gets distorted, but there is a process of corruption here. A warping in which thought is forced to chop everything up and reconstitute itself as sound bites. Strings of consumable ideas. So far as that image is concerned, like the image the New York artistic milieu – the Simulationists – reflected back to me, there's nothing you can do about it. It's an extension of what you do that's entirely beyond your control. Sometimes you just have to say to hell with it. But what I'm giving up on here isn't Bataille's 'accursed share'. I'm conceding something I'd rather not [*air of bitter amusement*].

THE CONSUMER SOCIETY: I'M A SITUATIONIST

MJ/HL *After* America, *do you regard yourself as a mentor of modernity or as an American tour guide?*

America was the test case. The reception of the book over there was catastrophic. That was a bit demoralising because I really liked *America*. It's a book in which I let things rip a bit . . . I didn't particularly hope it would be seen that way, but even so . . . As it happened, all the metaphors – desert, primal scene and so on – were taken literally. The critics were all of one mind, focusing exclusively on the ignorance of this Frenchman who knew nothing of the real America, didn't care about it anyway and was just hawking his European stereotypes around. The conclusion was that it wasn't a serious work. I took a bit of a battering.

There was plenty of reaction to the book, but a total refusal to engage with it. On the other hand, it was publicity. We're still stuck with the publicity syndrome – positive or negative.

MJ/HL *You say you're not responsible for your readers or for the images reflected back to you, but over your career, as a university professor who's appeared on the cover of* The Face, *haven't you felt that bridges have been burned, that there have been moments of transition, breaks with the past?*

I've always had the impression of advancing in a spiral movement – one single spiral. But the terms change, the hypotheses. There have perhaps been two breaks all the same: at the end of the 1970s (*Symbolic Exchange and Death*, 1976) and five years ago (*America*). I didn't have the impression I was seeing things in a different way. I haven't compromised or had second thoughts. Things have moved forward, but not in a way that was planned in advance. I've never worked with notes, card indexes or anything like that. The references have increasingly disappeared from my work. You could almost say I no longer work with any terms of comparison [*coldly*] . . . During the first period I was still operating in quite a specific, determinate cultural field – though less and less so. It isn't that I feel I've changed. My work has found channels for itself that I had no notion of. Art, for example. Aesthetics isn't my subject. Suddenly, visual artists became strangely enthusiastic about my writing.

MJ/HL *You speak of leaving out references. Aren't we talking there about a betrayal of academia?*

As for academia, I was always a traitor to it from the outset. I was never really part of it. I was in teaching because that was the only practical possibility. I never felt like a pedagogue, even if I didn't always find that role unpleasant. I'm not a researcher either. I was always split off from the educational institution. I played the renegade to some extent. The university authorities replied in kind and I didn't rise through the profession. And in fact that's all over now, I'm out of it. There were some good moments. It was good to be there in 1968. But I've simply passed through the university. I'd say the same of the wider intellectual milieu. There were people I liked – Sartre, then Barthes, but practically no one after that. I'm objectively part of that world and, if I don't have any references or role-models, I don't have any disciples, school or networks around me either. I've never had any followers inside the academic institution. This isn't betrayal, but a strategy of 'hanging loose' and of freedom that was there from the outset.

MJ/HL *But aren't you more exposed now than at the time when you were protected to some extent by an academic framework? When you published* The Consumer Society *in French, the jacket had the words 'Jean Baudrillard, Professor of Sociology' on it. That offers a little protection. Could you have imagined just launching yourself out there without any of that?*

That's not how I started. At 20 I was writing something different. Artaud, Rimbaud and Hölderlin were my thing [*Baudrillard contributed reviews to* Les Temps modernes]. At a pinch, Nietzsche and Bataille. But I wasn't involved in any kind of research. Then came the political, ideological period – Sartre and the Algerian war. After that, I dropped all the rest and went into discourse and practice. A plunge into theory at the age of 40. But my relation to more poetic language, let's call it, to less operational language – that's always been there. In a way I've just gone back to it. In the days of the grand ideologies, I did those things like everyone else. But when I wrote books like *The Consumer Society*, the only book I wrote to fulfil a commission – and the most extensive – I never thought that was the real deal. I had a much tighter, much denser relationship with language. I wasn't playing about in those books, the ones that are still discursive, explanatory and interpretative; it was a serious business. But it was never the be-all-and-end-all. Producing books like *The Consumer Society*, I was protected; I was part of a world. Having said that, when you're a sociologist of my sort, you end up with all of sociology ranged against you. The protection zone doesn't reach very far.

MJ/HL *Nevertheless, there's a clear break in the style of delivery of information – between books with a statistical apparatus and the others.*

The small quantity of statistics I've used in my life weren't incorrect, but they were entirely second-hand. I've never done that kind of work and wasn't capable of it. *The Consumer Society* is a book that relied on that kind of alibi. I have no special sources of information. I have access to the raw information that's available to everyone. I'm a Situationist in the sense that it really is situations that interest me – political situations, intimate situations. Every situation that provides an instant matrix of things. From there I move towards what is, to some extent, fiction.

Always starting out from some current event. I've roamed around in the history of ideas. However, I don't start out from that genealogy of ideas, but more from moments and objects. I've remained faithful to the object in the broadest sense of the word. The object and the surprise it provokes. The telescoping of a situation . . . fateful events [*mumbled*], but in their surprising, unpredictable implications. This is the, as it were . . . strategic point. After that, I have no method.

AMERICA: TRAVEL IS A WAY OF DISAPPEARING

MJ/HL *In* America, *you write: 'The point is not to write the sociology or psychology of the car, the point is to drive. That way you learn more about this society than all academia could ever tell you.'*[2]

It's better to have this roving eye, like a cinema tracking-shot . . . even in an empty space, if necessary. But that's the space where something always happens. What happens there is more interesting than what happens in pre-prepared, predetermined environments, where you always end up rehashing what was present in the model you started with. The search for other intersections always involves leaving the place you started from. Car driving is a metaphor, but it's something like that.

MJ/HL *Isn't there a danger of receiving things second-hand? To take a detail from* America, *you misspelled Jimi Hendrix's name . . .*

Yes, so I'm told. This level of unpredictability also produces *collage* and *bricolage*. It's perhaps clearer in a book like *America*. In *Cool Memories*, I almost make a principle out of it: using whatever happens – so long as it's something you're alive to, so long as it sparks something in your mind and makes an impact. There isn't good and bad material. I'm not checking things out beforehand, seeking potential coherence, but I'm not artificially creating incoherence either. There has to be a coherence that isn't the coherence of a field or subject [*matière*]. In that sense, my books can be disappointing. I ran up successively against the very reasonable opinions of economists and psychoanalysts. They all objected to everything. But to engage with those objections and try to answer them is to become a hostage to every discipline. And to get stuck. Thought isn't static or domestic; it doesn't belong to a particular *field* of thought. So what if I'm accused of infringing disciplinary boundaries? That's what I like doing. At least I've learned not to overdo things now. That's become a rule of life.

MJ/HL *To take some precise situations, when you were in America did you go to Stevie Wonder concerts or downtown to watch porn films?*

I dragged myself off to all those things. I don't do so much of that now. It was fifteen years ago.

MJ/HL *How did you get around?*

Always by car. Cars are all I know. And planes. That was the only way of travelling through that space. Perhaps it's the case that cars are entirely abstract. They're abstractions that allow you to drop anything any time.

MJ/HL *Was there whiskey in the car?*

Yes, that's right. Those things are constants.

MJ/HL *How do you choose the places? On the assumption that somewhere would have significance or just from a desire to go and take a look?*

No, not just the desire to go and take a look. First there's an affinity. With America that affinity was clear and present even before I went there. The journey in America wasn't calculated in advance. It was a spontaneous process, an unplanned encounter. I know Japan and Brazil. And those countries probably interest me more today, but I couldn't do a trip like I did in America again. A mental trip, a trip as theoretical as that one, would be impossible on another subject. I've had other ideas – to go off to Patagonia, for example. But that's already something that's been written about. Patagonia is so fashionable. So, too bad about Patagonia!

I use all my travelling for this kind of 'tracking shot' experience, obviously. I only go to places where I'm attracted by something unusual or new, avoiding repetition as much as possible. America's the only country I've been able to go to over a fifteen-year period where there's always something fresh, some new attraction or insight all the time. Though having said that . . .

MJ/HL *Do you come back with travel notebooks?*

My first travel notebook is from America and dates from the 1980s. My aim was to write as events dictated. There was a heatwave at the time and the air conditioning in the car had broken down. Even holding a notebook was out of the question. But the idea comes from that period. Afterwards, I went on writing little notebooks that travelled around with me. But the writing was very irregular. It wasn't day on day. There were breaks, moments when . . . as though my sensibility had switched off . . . nothing was worthy of note. You stop writing. That's how *Cool Memories 1980–85* came to a halt all on its own. I have to say that the memories weren't initially intended for publication. For two years I stopped, feeling curiously disaffected with the manuscript, remote from it. Then it started up again. But *Cool Memories 1987–90* is the last.

MJ/HL *Talking about the idea of travel, you mention the name of Rimbaud. If travel meant an end to writing for him, has it, for you, meant an end to thinking – that end towards which you say you're moving?*

What Rimbaud was about was a farewell to everything. It wasn't even about travel, but a spatial break with things and a break in his life. With me, travel gives me the mobility that enables me to think. If I don't move around, from time to time I sink into a kind of intellectual hypochondria. I'm not a continuous sort of thinker. Discontinuity has to be invented all the time. It isn't an end in itself to get to know peoples and countries in a realist sense. Instead I use travel as a strategy of deterritorialisation and acceleration. I derive energy from it each time. However, I've begun the process before I set off! The two things are necessary.

Travel is, after all, a way of disappearing. Though not in Rimbaud's sense, which is final and, ultimately, pathos-laden. It may become so, though. I don't know. There's always an obscure Rimbaud-type primal scene . . . Having said that, it's probably too late.

MJ/HL *You often range a past period against a present time. Are these the temporal divisions of the fashion magazine, where one season drives out another, or are we talking about historical or even mythic time, as in* Fatal Strategies (1983) *– the time of the gods and the time of men?*

These separations belong more to a mental schema than a real one. Primitive societies once served me as a reference myth. There was still a mythological idealism about that. Since then, it's been much less clear. Precisely as in myth, in fact, there's a break after the primal crime. It's always about the primal crime: whether it actually took place or not, it's there as the premise for the catastrophe or the end. Since then, there's been no nostalgia for mythology. That reference went out of my thinking when I moved to the idea of passing, at the very outset, beyond what I term the point of disappearance. What's involved here is accepting that the catastrophe has already happened – the same way primitive societies assume an origin in a crime – and then seeing what the new rules of the game are after that. With myth, our task is to interpret it, but it wasn't an interpretative system; it was more of an oracular, profanatory discourse. In attempting a language that doesn't lend itself to interpretation, do I get back to myth again? Possibly so, in the form of the fragment.

MJ/HL *Aren't you contributing to a certain vagueness as soon as you begin a paragraph with 'It's amusing to think . . .'? When you say, 'The man of today is inferior to his own masculine essence',*[3] *what do you mean by 'today'?*

Sexuality? Have things really changed? We just don't know. Between male and female there's a plane of reversibility, the plane of seduction. This is an indestructible form. And another plane of astonishing wave patterns where effects of anteriority and ulteriority are created. But there, feminine and masculine are no longer understood in the same sense. They're no longer forms but cultural and moral anatomical complexes. That's something else. One's forced to operate in these two registers and they're not always adequate.

MJ/HL *You speak rather interestingly of the passing of your colleagues Lacan, Foucault, and Barthes, who died, you say, of their philosophy of disappearance. Derrida is holding on well!*

Yes, yes, exactly [*laughter*] . . . And me too, I'm holding on OK – by disappearing. Derrida, Lyotard, and I belong, perhaps, to a generation that's living well from philosophy. They aren't so caught up in this process of disappearance. There's a re-establishment of a philosophising form of thought. The philosophy in question is conservative in the special sense that it's able to live on – and to do so very well. That's clear. As I see it, this is a way of distinguishing between two different kinds of thought. Those that don't live on work themselves out fully and then disappear. And not just in philosophy; Warhol's a case of this too. He dies at the moment he should die. There's real drama to this new dimension of thought – disappearance – which has entered the destinies of a certain number of people. If pressed, I'd say there's a certain beauty to it. It's rather grander, at any rate, than those philosophies that do very well out of their continuity – while speaking all the time of their discontinuity and difference – and out of the accumulation of their own discourse. I don't know which I belong to; in my heart, I see myself more in the first group.

FORGET BAUDRILLARD: IT FOLLOWS LOGICALLY THAT YOU SHOULD ALSO WITHDRAW YOURSELF FROM THE GAME

MJ/HL *You say that to come home from Los Angeles is to land back in the nineteenth century. Yet here in your sitting room, doesn't everything revolve, once again, around the bourgeois dream of 1789?*

I moved in here three years ago, but I can genuinely say that the decoration isn't my doing. To me, it's like a hotel suite in a strange town. I was better off before, over Bastille way, in a space with no qualities. I've never found a form of dwelling or decor that matches the image of a place I could live in. I don't have that image. Objects are a mental obsession of mine, but in real life I'm almost indifferent to them. A project of inhabiting a space is something that's been beyond me. I don't feel responsible for my surroundings.

MJ/HL *Do you draw a distinction between talking about what you see and talking about yourself? For example, aren't the viral metaphors in your recent texts talking about your body, about fear associated with that body today?*

No, my writing didn't come out of a reality of that kind, a reality of intimate concern to me. We're not talking about private or introspective journals – though there may be a sort of presentiment of something. Certainly, afterwards, where writing's concerned, it becomes existential. Writing functions like a kind of . . . not to be too overblown about it . . . destiny. At a certain point, simulation, seduction, virality – and also *life* – are engendered from there. Was it writing that played a role? I don't think you can separate things out like that. They're inextricably linked. I'll never know to what extent I'm in there, but I'm not there in psychological terms, even in the notebooks. The 'I' isn't psychological. I'm not telling my own story in the episodes that come over. I actually believe one should keep well away from the weakness of a lot of current literature. Justifying something by lived experience is weak [*forthright tone*].

MJ/HL *Reading you, the thought occurred of a self-induced disappearance of the 'historian of the snows'*[4] *that you claim to be.*

Yes, but you're talking about something staged. If such a disappearance did occur, you wouldn't know anything about it and nor would I. Last summer, I almost passed away in a common little accident. I was teetering over a ravine. Things could have ended there in a rather mundane way.

MJ/HL *Can you imagine being invisible?*

Yes [*laughter*] . . . absolutely. But how do you conceive of that? I think writing's already a way of concealing your voice, of getting back to a sort of secrecy. Some people produce visibility, others secrecy. My writing's more in the vein of recreating secrecy. Admittedly, it's like the animal digging its own burrow: in the end, it's in there and there it stays. Logically, if there were a fulfilment of desire, that would be it. After withdrawing concepts from thought and words from the language, it follows logically that you should also withdraw yourself from the game, should let the 'I' not wreck the game but withdraw from it as an invisible actor – to merge with the rules of the game almost.

MJ/HL *The rules of the game?*

The functioning of illusion. The rule of the world is illusion – total illusion. The world operates with apparently secret rules which aren't, in any way, to do with reality. It's a game, but there's a set of rules. My entire analysis of the simulacrum is based on the fact that an attempt is being made to escape the world as illusion. The Cathars, in their day, and lots of people thought of the world as illusion. That was how everyone thought except us: that you can have the symbolic mastery of illusion, not the technical mastery of reality. It isn't entirely new . . . For some reason or another, this illusion scares us. It's unbearable. The trick we've hit on for escaping it consists in *realising* the world – or, in other words, putting an end to the illusion of the world through technology. That's what simulation is about, as I see it. We're talking here about simulation versus illusion. If there's an alternative to simulation today – though it's difficult to conceive of one – it certainly isn't reality, since that's the same thing. It's illusion.

Translated by Chris Turner

NOTES

1. J. Baudrillard (1990), *Cool Memories*, London: Verso, p. 159.
2. J. Baudrillard (1988), *America*, London: Verso, p. 54.
3. J. Baudrillard (1996), *Cool Memories II, 1987–90*, Cambridge: Polity, p. 27. [Editors]
4. J. Baudrillard (1996), *Cool Memories II, 1987–90*, Cambridge: Polity, p. 13. [Editors]

2 Disappearance beyond Disappearance

Interview with Catherine Francblin (CF)

CF *You are one of the most frequently quoted French thinkers by those in the contemporary art scene. Critics use your texts as commentary on the work of artists, and artists cite your texts as an apology for their work. How do you feel about this?*

I like it of course. Because of the ambiguity of my relationship with the university, I am pleased that my work operates in other areas. I noticed in Berlin, and in Australia as well, that the prominent figures in the plastic arts or in performance had taken over my books, often in the most unorthodox manner. But to tell the truth, I did not meet them. When I was in New York I went to the galleries, but I hardly had any occasion to talk with the artists.

CF *A new generation of abstract geometrical artists, who appeared in the States in the early 1980s, is very close to your line of thought. Peter Halley, who is also a writer, has said: 'Reading Baudrillard is the equivalent for me of looking at a painting by Andy Warhol.'*

Ah, Warhol! For me he meant a great deal as well. I must have mentioned him when I was interested in Pop art and Hyperrealism. What I liked about Warhol was his approach to the series, his irony, his decision to abolish art. I believe that he was one of the only people at that time capable of rendering the idea of the 'machine'. With a personal elegance and great severity, he designed a playing field for logical anarchy that is quite remarkable. I was also interested in the Velvet Underground at the end of the 1960s and beginning of the 1970s. However, the only work of mine which deals explicitly with art is a text on gesture and signature.[1]

CF *It seems to me that you never refer to individual artists.*

That's true, I have never chosen a religious canon for art. I took whatever came along. However after Pop art and Hyperrealism, it seemed to me that there was not much more to be said, at least as far as the problematics of the simulacra go – problematics which, after all, are rather old stuff for me. After that, I scarcely found any new ideas as far as the logical history of the form and image goes. That just about wound things up, even if all sorts of variations, mannerisms, and extreme positions were to follow.

CF *The so-called 'Neo-Geos', as the geometrists of New York are called, no longer believe that Warhol represents a sort of purity or truth in art. They use an abstraction of quotations.*

Generally speaking, playing with quotations is boring for me. I can understand that postmodernism, intertextuality and so on can cause a vertigo, but in my opinion that is far from constituting a high-water mark and it is never a goal in itself! The infinite nesting of box within box, the game of second- and third-degree quotes, I think that is a pathological form of the end of art, a sentimental form. It would be more exciting for me to find something beyond the vanishing point: a hyper-simulation which would be a type of disappearance beyond disappearance. That is what I tried to hypothesise with the term *fatal*. If only art could accomplish the magic act of its own disappearance! But it continues to make believe it is disappearing when it is already gone. Perhaps art today is struggling in the shadow of the threat of the phenomenon of the 'new images', just like painting did in relation to photography. On the other hand, on the horizon of simulation, I was interested in something else – seduction. I do not believe that seduction is what is at stake in art today. Art seems, in fact, to have nothing at stake at all.

CF *After having transparency for a criterion – I'm thinking of the Demonstrative Art of the 1970s – today's art confesses, on the contrary, to a refusal of understanding. A French painter like [Gérard] Garouste, who was a conceptual artist, declares today: 'We are not out to understand.'*

The secret of seduction, however, does not lie in the recreation of a sort of *trompe l'oeil* opacity! Hiding things, disguise, has nothing to do with simulation! What we need is a new set of rules for the game. In spite of the fact that I am quoted as a postmodernist, I consider that the major ideas of our times, in art, philosophy, politics and elsewhere, date from the first twenty or thirty years of the century. There was a breakthrough, late in the 1960s and 1970s, especially in the area of theory – which brought about a diffusion of the discoveries of the beginning of the century. But postmodernism – if that is what we call the following period – seems to me to be an inferior time. Our period seems to me the poorest ever imaginatively, and people are subletting the leftovers of the strong ideas from the beginning of the century. Perhaps a culture is obliged to go through a process of garbage disposal? At any rate, that is what is going on now. Intelligence and subtlety are great indeed, but strong ideas are lacking.

CF *In the system of circulating signs that you describe, death is extremely present.*

I tried to make of it a stake at the basis of an indefinite game. Another thing that I was trying to say is that an enormous energy can come from the disappearance itself. Take Nietzsche – he could still write a genealogy of morals and find in the death of God a mythical vision beyond this death. For us, God is not dead; he has disappeared, that's all. The act of disappearance is often an intense one, and I see the 1960s and the 1970s as this strong point during which, out of the consciousness of disappearance, people took all the energy they could. We witnessed the disappearance of a great number of concepts, of forms, of ancient myths. Now, we no longer even have the work of mourning to go through; all that remains is a state of melancholia. The high point of the disappearance was situated between Nietzsche and the 1920s–1930s. People like Canetti or Benjamin lived through both the high point of a culture and the high point of its decline. Today, we see the result of this process of decline and everyone is wondering how to make a drama out of that. Personally, the only rebound that I found was America. Through a sort of displacement, I succeeded in seeing the phenomenon of the disappearance of our culture in a more grandiose, intense and spectacular version. That is something like what de Tocqueville noticed. He had witnessed in France the disappearance of aristocratic values and the setting-up of a revolution-restoration which half-failed. However he thought that over there in America, where these values had never existed, they had at least disappeared from the beginning, and that fact could perhaps produce more impressive results than what he saw in France. As a matter of fact, through a transference, America offered me the possibility of grasping the loss of our bourgeois values and of our culture, everything which has disappeared here, as a rather exceptional event. A spontaneous, general desire exists to act as though there were still some culture, some common values, and so on. That is easy to observe in politics: a whole political class acts as if there were still a political ideology. Can this culture of sorts, this *trompe l'oeil*, be maintained much longer? Does the regeneration of sentimental and affective values, even in politics with the Rights of Man, with SOS this and that, have any real foundation? In my opinion, this is no more than a completely formalistic sort of solidarity which is meant to produce the illusion of a social link, of the participation of everyone for the same objective. Even Coluche, the French comedian and social critic, has participated in this effort. But it is impossible to ignore that, behind it all, there is not a great deal. So perhaps the only alternative is to negotiate one's indifference as art does, as art has been negotiating its disappearance for half a century. People, artists, are not just dying in their corner; they are making their disappearance an object of exchange.

CF *You speak of indifference towards cultural values. Isn't an exhibition like the Viennese one at the Pompidou Centre a sign of non-indifference; the sign of an interest, even a passion for the past?*

If it is, it's a posthumous passion! This passion for the past is for me something like redemption rather than predestination. The past is not fatal, it does not oblige us to do anything. This spiritual dramatisation of our memory goes along with the new technology which can only be used to stock information, which blots out memory. 'Memories' are what work best nowadays! But computers do not produce a new vision of the world; the system is only a vast machine which allows for the development of compilation. Indifference: that's an ambiguous word. It has a negative connotation for us. However, when the Stoics used it, it was dynamic. The indifference of nature produced a sort of challenge to the world. They did not experience indifference as a flat encephalogram, but rather as a tragic condition to which one must reply with an indifference at least as great. All sorts of things can happen around the category of indifference – seduction, for example, because the play of seduction always includes a moment of play with desire, or the refusal of desire. I usually speak ironically of desire. Indifference implies, for me, that 'something is involved'. In my opinion, we must make of indifference a stake, a strategy: dramatise it. Why not consider indifference as the 'damned portion'? Be that as it may, I do not believe that we can go to the past in search of lost values. Postmodernism registers the present situation, the loss of meaning and of desire, the mosaic-like aspect of things, but it does not make of decadence a grandiose event. To do that, one would need to be a mediator, in writing perhaps: an object which would be provoking in its very indifference.

CF *In the realm of today's arts, the objective is often to create modulators of the environment. When it leaves meaning behind, art tends sometimes to approach the decorative.*

Is it worthwhile trying to find the meaning of the setting? For the dramatisation of what? Who will the new playwrights and new actors be? Everyone seems to be saying, 'I am setting up a new stage, but in this space, in this new light, no one will ever move; there will be no play.' That is rather the way I see the environment of Buren at the Palais Royal: a stage set in another set. That always seems to me to be a part of the aesthetics of ruins. The actors have disappeared; only the backstage and parts of the stage sets remain!

Translated by Nancy Blake

NOTE

1. J. Baudrillard (1981), *For a Critique of the Political Economy of the Sign*, St Louis: Telos, pp. 102–11. [Editors]

3 After Utopia: The Primitive Society of the Future

Interview with Nathan Gardels (NG)

NG *You have called America the 'primitive society of the future'. What do you mean?*

Like primitive societies of the past, America doesn't have a past. It has no 'ancestral territory' – speaking not of land but of symbolic terrain – that has accumulated centuries of meaning and cultivated principles of truth. In short, America has no roots except in the future and is, therefore, nothing but what it imagines. It is perpetual simulation. America has no context other than what it, concretely, is. From a historical standpoint, America is weightless . . .

NG *The 'lightness of being' on a grand scale!*

Exactly. Like primitive societies, America lives primarily in nature and the unconscious realm of myths and symbols. America is only nature and artificiality, space plus a spirit of fiction. There is no self-reflexive, self-mirroring level, the civilising level of unhappy consciousness, which comes with history and which places a distance between the symbolic and the real. It is this lack of distance and lack of capacity for ironic reflection that accounts for America's naïve and primitive qualities. Without knowledge of irony, the imaginary and the real are fused and indistinguishable. Disneyland is authentic! Television and movies are real! America has created an ideal world from nothing and consecrated it in the cinema.

NG *This absence of critical distance is also reflected, wouldn't you say, in the aesthetic nausea of the built environment in Los Angeles – the freeways, the commercial strips with their signs competing for the attention of mobile consumers, with each building architecturally unrelated to the others?*

America is beyond aesthetics. It is transaesthetical, like a desert. Culture exists in a wild state where all aesthetics are sacrificed in a process of literal transcription of dreams into reality. In the car ads, for example, there is no difference between the car and happiness. In the mind of the consumer, the material reality of the car and the metaphysical concept of happiness and contentment are identical. A car is happiness. Who could ask for anything more than a new Toyota? Aesthetics requires context, and in America the only context is its own mythic banality.

In Europe, we philosophise on the end of lots of things. It is in America, though, that we should look for the ideal type of the end of our culture.

NG *The medium is the myth, so to speak. How, then, is America 'utopia achieved', as you have put it?*

Well, what did the European philosophers expect utopia to look like? America is, in concrete form, the traumatic consequence of European dreams. America is the original version of modernity, the weightless paradise of liberation from the past. Europe is the dubbed or subtitled version. What is only thought in Europe becomes reality in America. It is we who imagine that everything culminates in transcendence, and that nothing exists that hasn't been conceptualised. Americans are not interested in conceptualising reality but in materialising ideas.

NG *'Don't let us get too deep', as Edie Brickell sings.*

Americans inhabit true fiction by giving it the form of reality, while we are condemned to the imaginary and to nostalgia for the future. We anticipate reality by imagining it, or flee from it by idealising it. Americans merely radically implement everything we think about, from mass egalitarianism to individualism to freedom to fantasy. In so doing, 'utopia achieved' has transformed into the anti-utopia of unreason, weightlessness, value neutralism, indifference, the indeterminacy of language, and the death of culture. Having hyperrealised modernity, the hyperreality turns against modernity.

America was 'deconstructed' from the outset because of its original inauthenticity – the utopian moral sphere has always been your primal scene, while history and politics remain ours. California, in particular, is the world centre of the inauthentic. As the scene of anti-utopia, its vitality is the mirror of our decadence.

NG *The vitality of Los Angeles springs from weightlessness. The cultural indifference is precisely what enables the new wave of Third World immigrants, who have left their ancestral territory, to build their own particular utopia inside the anti-utopia. I'm thinking here not only of the Mexican and Korean immigrants, but especially of the Vietnamese boat people who have reconstructed a mini-Saigon in the shadow of Disneyland's fake Matterhorn.*

These emigrants from real space to hyperreality reinforce the American model. They are complex hybrids of origin and artificiality. In this powerful simulacrum of California, they are giving the form of reality to their fiction.

NG *In Los Angeles, it is possible to touch the living, breathing hybridity and fragmentation of cultural life, the deconstructed and decentred diaspora so eloquently theorised upon in Parisian salons. But tell me this: what accounts for Europe's craving for American inauthenticity? We export it by the boatload. Our consecrated fictional realism plays in most Parisian movie theatres, McDonald's graces the Champs Elysée, and Disneyland has opened just outside Paris. How can simulated inauthenticity be so appealing?*

We are both attracted to American mass culture and repelled by it. We still have enough distance to be fascinated by, rather than inhabit, its factitiousness.

But the resistance is fragile. We don't have anything to oppose to this cultural contamination. Culturally and philosophically exhausted, we remain unable to transform our past into living values for the present. Our cultural antibodies have acquired an immune deficiency, and can't resist the virus.

NG *Isn't the name of that immune deficiency syndrome 'indifference'? Marcel Duchamp noted long ago that the ultimate face of modernity was this 'freedom of indifference'.*

In Europe at least, a sense of loss still accompanies indifference. But in America, indifference is already anachronistic. The strategy of indifference was there from the start. In fact, America's genius, as Alexis de Tocqueville noted in both horror and admiration, was the irrepressible abolition of difference. Sheltered from the vicissitudes of history far from its shores, America was indifferent to the world. Inside its boundaries, the radical form of its indifference became the toleration of any and all differences.

In the end, this is what the universal cultural problematic of deconstruction is all about. Without a centre, without a transcendent context, how do you value differences?

Thanks to the hegemony of the West, indifference has become a universal fact. In the future, power will belong to those peoples with no origins and no authenticity. It will belong to those who, like America from the beginning, can achieve 'deterritorialisation' and weightlessness and figure out how to exploit the situation to the full extent. Whether we like it or not, the future has shifted away from any historical centre towards artificial satellites.

The unintelligible paradox of Japan is a powerful example of this. Having freed itself from the ancestral terrain, it floats, culturally weightless, as an economic powerhouse on the world scene.

NG *Your vision of the world sounds like Salman Rushdie's: a world of uprooted migrants, fragments, debris of the soul, bits and pieces from here and there – all with a hole inside, 'a vacancy in the vital inner chamber'. In your terms, weightless, indifferent satellites floating unattached about the planet. Rushdie's vision, however, was challenged from the quarters of the centred absolute, the ultimate face of the anti-modern: Khomeini.*

I agree with Rushdie that the whole world is implicated in this fragmentation and uprootedness, including China and Russia. There is one exception: Islam. It stands as a challenge to the radical indifference sweeping the world.

NG *It seems that all these weightless fragments are juxtaposed, living side by side in ontological uncertainty without mixing . . .*

And that is unstable. Perhaps that is why the West is so weak and vulnerable in the face of the certitudes of radical Islam.

In a way, radical Islam is the revenge of modern history. The West inoculated them with our virus, and now they are immune to us. So now, people like Ayatollah Khomeini can contaminate the whole Western world with terrorism and death threats.

Khomeini's question about the West is perhaps also ours: what happens after the great orgy of freedom that has left us all indifferent?

NG *In effect, what comes after utopia?*

Perhaps reversibility. The march of history has broken from its forward path. It seems anything can happen beyond this point, good or bad. We can't live with the past, but neither do we have a project. Every day is rich with unpredictable happenings: terrorism, AIDS, electronic viruses . . . the course is uncharted.

NG *Man's fate has checked into purgatory.*

Well, Europe, at least, still survives in the purgatory of simulation. We still harbour a vague regret over the loss of origins and are wary of the inauthentic. Americans are in the paradise of simulation, long comfortable with weightlessness as a way of life.

For Europe, there may be no way from purgatory to paradise. And that could be our salvation.

© 'After Utopia: The Primitive Society of the Future', *New Perspectives Quarterly* 6(2), Summer 1989, 52–4.

4 The Possibility of Another Game

Interview with Judith Williamson (JW)[1]

JW *You've said that theory should be rigorous enough to cut itself off from any system of reference* (Forget Foucault). *If you still think that, then what is the status of your theories – what do they explain?*

Yes, it's still true, more and more so in fact: in a way, theory has moved further and further from having a system of reference, which is the same as a critical system. What I mean is that traditionally, critical thought, analytical thought, has always needed a system of reference, and I had some for a long time – Marx, Freud and so on, like many others, and I had older references like Nietzsche, Hölderlin – then after a while I thought that one had to jump, to pass over to the other side of the line and lose a sense of reference in order for one's thought to be more a projection, an anticipation. And at that point theory gives way entirely to its object, to its object in a pure state. The subject of theory or of knowledge no longer seeks to interpret; we move away from interpretation and we come much closer to fiction. We have something which is more like a fiction-theory. So we have a theory which is no longer referenced; but of course, it's a paradox because there is always a kind of actuality, a reality, so we're talking about the reference being actuality, or even an anticipation of actuality. But it would come from the object itself, the events themselves, from situations themselves – so you have a kind of Situationism.

The term 'reference' bothers me because if you mean authors, theorists and so on, of course there are lots, there's been Sartre, Barthes, Marcuse, people like that, but that's something else. For myself, I'm talking not so much in terms of references, but in terms of the object. I think that theory is not so much a kind of lineage of references, a continuity, but rather a confrontation, an antagonism, a kind of duel between the object and theory, between the real and theory. So it's no longer so much the real or reality as a reference, but rather the reference would be the confrontation itself, the antagonism between the object and the theory. I don't think that the purpose of theory is to reflect reality, nor do I think its reference should be the history of ideas. We need something more adventurous, more direct, more aggressive if you like.

JW *You characterise systems of signification in our culture as circuits of signifiers with no referent. That seems very accurately to describe certain forms of imagery which endlessly refer to one another, like TV and advertising. But do you believe that holds true for all forms of signification, including writing, and in that case how do you see the function of writing?*

Yes, it is also true for a system of writing, for a theoretical system. All signs enter into such circuits, none escape – even theory itself becomes on some level a flow of signifiers with no referent. And this can be seen as negative in relation to classical theory, but it can be a very original situation. Theory then speaks of simulation but also offers itself *as* a system of simulation; and theory like mine doesn't claim to be anything more than *one* of the possible systems of simulation of something. I don't know what this theory signifies but there is an act by which it traces its own object, it attempts to be an analogue, or a homologue, of that object. So if you're speaking of simulation you have to hold a discourse *of* simulation. If you're speaking of seduction, you have to hold a discourse *of* seduction, and so on. There is a kind of osmosis, almost a resemblance, an identification of theory with its object. Which means that it becomes its own reference. It becomes a kind of pure object or a pure event. Writing remains this kind of pure event, something like an act. And I don't just mean the workings of language – there is something more in the fact of writing: there is no difference today between the state of things and the state of theory. There is a kind of short circuit, an implosion between the two. Whereas in critical theory there is a distance between discourse and reality.

JW *You've shown how Marx privileges use-value in the same way that theories of signification privilege the referent. But challenging that privilege is not necessarily the same as denying that there* is *any use-value or referent, i.e. the material world.*

My criticism of use-value or of the referent is of course a challenge to reference, a challenge to the material world, or rather, a challenge to the *principle* of reality, because the reality principle is at some level a principle of reference. In order for there to be a reality, there has to be a principle of reference, a principle of signification, a principle of reality. Yes, I do contest it. There is a challenge there [in my work] to all that, including the use of language: in a way I'm also doing a critique of the use-value of language. So in this case theory no longer aims solely to signify something, or certainly it doesn't exhaust itself in the process of signification. It has to invent another object, it has to invent another world as it were; it does have a kind of strength, a power which is almost utopian, or maybe it's more the power of paradox, a position of paradox that we're talking about. And in the paradox there is the fact that reality becomes ambiguous, paradoxical, certainly undecidable – so it no longer has a functional use-value: one can no longer say, this is real, this is rational, this is true. So then theory is forced to evolve in a universe of contingency – which is a universe of simulation and so on. So it's a big game, isn't it? – a gamble. It's a game, but there are rules.

JW *Your writing suggests that there is no space outside the hyperreal but you say that 'it's essential today to evaluate the double challenge of the masses and their silence, and of the media'* ('The Masses', 1985).[2] *What do you see as the space from which such an evaluation might take place?*

It's no longer the traditional space, no longer the critical space where there would be a historical contradiction, a contradiction of meaning. This hyperreal space which has no depth – which is therefore superficial – is no longer a mirror: it's a screen. It's the space of the screen. And the masses themselves are a screen. Their answer, their silence, their reverberation of all the messages, the media and so on, has the function of a screen. But it's the function of an opaque screen whereas that whole system [of the media and so on] aims at a transparency of things. So the masses are a kind of opaque screen which no longer returns meaning – which absorbs meanings and no longer throws them back. It's a screen-space we're talking about; I can't put it any other way. A screen is a pure surface and at the same time it's a space. To look at it in different terms, in America you have the desert: the desert is also a pure space but completely superficial and it no longer sends back meaning. So there a circuit of meaning does indeed get cut.

So of course there is no longer any possibility of evaluation. It's an operation that's taking place, a kind of implosion of meaning. There isn't any point of view external to that space from which to criticise it.

There's a kind of immanence of the hyperreal and we are all caught in it: there's a kind of confusion of the negative and positive poles – there are no longer any intellectual positions in the traditional sense. There are no longer any positions of knowledge or evaluation which are outside the hyperreal, and it's that fact which constitutes the end of critical analysis. It's not possible to make a judgement. When I describe hyperreality or the media or whatever, there is no positive or negative judgement – well, maybe from time to time! – but in principle, there is no judgement, neither of morality nor of truth. I remain in the same ambivalence, if you like, as that space itself. So when people say to me, this work is pessimistic or it's optimistic, no, it's neither optimistic nor pessimistic, but I myself am making a hyperreal theory, about the hyperreal space.

JW *But in* America *you say, for example, of Reaganism, 'This consensus around simulation is much less fragile than is commonly thought since it is far less exposed to any testing against political truth'. What do you see as a political truth against which a simulation might be tested?*

Well, I mean 'political truth' in inverted commas, because it's what one imagines to be political reality, political contradictions, conflicts and so on. And simulation manages to neutralise conflicts. It manages to neutralise this political reality – the word reality isn't perhaps very appropriate – but in the universe of simulation there are no longer any contradictions. It's not a dialectical superseding, of course, but a neutralisation by means of simulation. So that's the problem. In the beginning I, too, made an analysis of simulation which was still a critical analysis, saying that this universe of simulation is a mystifying universe, an alienating universe – it's still alienation through the sign. But later, no, I don't think so. Simulation is no longer alienation, we pass into something else and from there on one is no longer confronted by the political state of things. We are in a universe of simulation – it's the smile of Reagan – it can also be the cancer of Reagan! Because the cancer of Reagan is as simulated, in the theoretical sense of the term, as the smile of Reagan. It's the same thing.

JW *So do you see any possibility for a strategy that could oppose the system of capital?*

I'm not a strategist, I don't hold out any political alternatives. I no longer see any political alternatives. The alternative – I've already described it – is a kind of strategy of indifference. The universe of simulation is an indifferent universe, a neutralised one: and it's the same strategy on the other side, on the side of the masses. People do in fact defend themselves, they have defensive and even offensive strategies, but this time through indifference. Which is to say, they don't fight any more through difference, through demands, through struggle and conflict, but on the contrary, they turn the system back on itself according to its own weapons, its own logic – they fight with the same weapons as the system itself. And therefore we're no longer in the same political universe; we are in a universe I call transpolitical, or something like that. There is still something at stake, there is still an antagonism, there is certainly a struggle between the strategy of simulation at the level of political power, or what is left of political power, and a strategy of indifference, which is to say that the masses also manage to neutralise power, but by their silence, by their indifference. It's no longer a strategy of subversion.

JW *But you're not silent.*

No [*laughs*]. That's paradox [*laughs*]. The strategy is no longer, as it was in the classical political world, the strategy of negativity – for example – of subversion, the negativity of revolution; the transpolitical world is more analogous to a game of poker, if you like, where there is a raising of the stakes: where you outbid indifference with indifference. You up a bid of neutralisation with more neutralisation. So it becomes a game at this point; it's become something else. It is no longer exactly a historical or political space.

JW *How do you place your theoretical development in relation to the political movements of the sixties? You mentioned Situationism. How do you see your work in relation to it, and has that relationship changed?*

My work really has its roots in the movements of the sixties. In France there were lots: there were the Situationists, there was *Socialisme ou Barbarie*, we ourselves had started a journal called *Utopie* – there were all those movements. For my part I'd say it's very definitely from the sixties that this kind of theory was born, and 1968 was absolutely determining, it was crucial for the position of theory. For me particularly, I was very, very attracted by Situationism. I wasn't part of the movement but yes, Situationism is like a kind of primitive theoretical scene, a radical one. And even if today Situationism is past, there remains a kind of radicality to which I have always been faithful. There is a kind of obsession, a kind of counterculture, which is still there. Something that has really stayed with me – and that's why I am not at bottom a philosopher, it's because I have always had a kind of radical suspicion towards culture, or even towards ideas – a kind of barbarism, in fact. A barbarian position [*laughs*].

JW *You say in your latest book that America is 'suffering from the disappearance of ideologies that might contest its power'. Do you think that your work is symptomatic of that situation?*

Yes, I think there is a kind of homology with the American situation, the American state of things. In fact since the sixties I have thought that it was at bottom the American reality, or the American hyperreality, which was the model, the anticipation, the fiction of our own ideas; and it's true that what I've done is a little bit the same. Which is to say that in the same way that America ultimately takes European utopias or European ideas to the end of their logic, realises them, materialises them, and by the same token neutralises them, that's a little of what I do in the field of theory. To take concepts all the way to their limits, to their extremities and even beyond their limits. So I try to realise them, and thereby I make them pass into fiction. I create a void, in a sense. And for me America is to some extent a strategy of the void, of emptiness, the desert. But not in a depressive way, not at all depressive – on the contrary, in a very prodigious way. So in the field of theory I have tried also to preserve this energy of the void, this energy of the realised utopia, an energy of something which passes into its own hyperlogic. For me, America is in fact a hyperlogical world; hyperreal because hyperlogical. The Americans did everything: what the Europeans thought, the Americans did. It's a kind of radical pragmatism, which forces one to throw into question anew all the ideas, all European idealism. So I too did that for theory. I think it's exactly the same thing.

JW *You say that the work of Marx fits perfectly the capitalist system which is its object: it colludes or collaborates with that system. Do you see your work as in some way symptomatic of and collaborative with late twentieth-century consumer capitalism?*

Yes, I think so, but this may be a pretension on my part. There is indeed a strong coincidence between the work of Marx and a certain state of capitalism, and I hope there is the same coincidence between my theories, if you like, and the post-Marxist state of things . . . I'm not sure if it's still capitalism, but in any case, the contemporary state of things. But it is symptomatic in the ambiguous sense of the word symptom, which is to say a symptom is at the same time something which translates a pathology – it produces a sign, it's the sign of a pathology, of a conflict – and at the same time it's a kind of sublimation of the pathology, it's also a kind of neurosis. A symptom is, in the end, a small neurosis which acts, not as a therapy, but all the same it's an event which contributes to precipitating the situation, not to find a solution but to go further in the situation. The symptom isn't just a sign which reflects an illness but it is an event *in* the illness. So theory would in that sense be symptomatic. It is ambivalent. It's negative inasmuch as it participates in a kind of pathology of reality and it's positive inasmuch as it tries to turn this reality into something else. So yes, in that sense symptomatic could be the right word.

JW *At one point when we were talking earlier you said that in* America *you were trying to explain something. Do you see your writing as interpretation, or seduction (to use your own terms)?*

Yes, more like a seduction. It's not an interpretation inasmuch as there isn't a meaning. I don't think of myself as a subject capable of interpreting America. America is an object which is too immense – it's beyond interpretation. On the other hand, and precisely because it's beyond interpretation, there is a fascination; fascination is a passion which remains beyond interpretation. It's not exactly seduction, it's more fascination. America is more fascinating than seductive. Seduction is – something else. And in describing America – well it's not a description, but in my sort of camera-movement over America – what I wanted to preserve was this fascination. Which remains always enigmatic. Interpretation seeks to be no longer enigmatic, to resolve the enigma. Whereas I seek to preserve the enigma – the enigma of America. And the enigma is seductive. It's fascinating, and seductive.

JW *What do you make of the cult status of your work, particularly among young people, in Britain, North America and Australia?*

I am a little surprised because you speak of a cult, which suggests that people are very interested in this – or perhaps fascinated – while on the other hand I have noticed that the critics, journalists and so on are almost all negative, they come up with negative criticisms. The official reaction of 'thinking people' or 'cultured people' is very often defensive, reticent – in short negative in one way or another. When it comes down to it, they can't bear this exposé of surface-ness, of non-reference and so on – they just can't bear it. I suppose there's nothing to be done about that. But maybe indeed young people are less concerned with questions of truth and criticism; they are more directly sensitive to this kind of writing which is fragmented, maybe also to the kind of game with superficiality – which is not necessarily a superficial game. It is a game with superficiality. Perhaps young people are more immediately sensitive to that, they haven't a defensive system of prejudices – so maybe it goes down better with them. But when I'm told this I find it very problematic, because it means, ultimately, that young people are ready to become fans like that – whereas what I speak about, I do claim that it is serious. It doesn't try to be deep, but still, there is at some level a kind of depth to it all. So for me it does remain enigmatic, why it should be so successful in that way. And it's often surprising that in New York, for example, the success is not with university students and academics but with artists and all that New York scene. I'm very pleased about that, it's rather nice, because I never particularly courted the university world – but I would have thought there could possibly be an acknowledgement from the field of philosophy, from the direction of the universities and so on, a little more recognition, and that it wouldn't just be a cultural or countercultural special effect. It's something else than that. But there it is, you can't control things.

JW *But perhaps the fatalism in your work corresponds to something – a political depression – that here, for example, under Thatcher, people actually feel? A desperation?*

Ah yes, here you have Thatcher. But I think that the atmosphere, the state of things, is somewhat the same in France, even if we have a kind of socialist government – I think the problem of political despair is everywhere. And of course there is a correspondence between what I speak about and this situation which is depressive, but what I am saying is not depressive; I try to cross over to the other side of this political depression through a kind of transpolitical analysis which would be, OK, not optimistic, definitely not optimistic, which would be – I'm not sure how to put it – fatal, but it's not fatalism in the passive sense: it's the idea that there is the possibility of another game. Another set of rules. You have to search for it, of course – it's precisely *not* despair – it's not hope but it's not despair either. Things are already happening differently now, there's definitely something else than the classic history of the political scene, because that is indeed in a bad way, it's depressive. But beyond this line of depression I think there is something else going on, something else is possible. Basically, one must not obstinately try to regenerate the political scene because I think that *is* without hope. In reality it's true my work reflects a kind of, yes, a kind of depression, of disappearance, and at the same time it's an attempt to transfigure all that in an energetic way, in a fictional way. To say, well, if it's another game, then let's play the other game. What I'm trying to say, in a nutshell, is if the work testifies to the disappearance of something, the loss of something, to a depression, I think that there is an energy of disappearance and this energy must be found. It's a bit like that. We're going to have to stop because I have to make a phone call.

Translated by Brand Thumim and Judith Williamson

NOTES

1. The corrections and amendments made to the original published version of this interview were made in correspondence with Judith Williamson. [Editors]
2. A reference to J. Baudrillard (1985), 'The Masses: The Implosion of the Social in the Media', *New Literary History* 16(3), Spring, pp. 577–89. Also see J. Baudrillard (1994), *Simulacra and Simulation*, Ann Arbor: University of Michigan Press, pp. 83–4. [Editors]

5 Politics of Performance: Montand, Coluche = Le Pen?

Interview with Pierre Archard (PA)

PA *What do you think of the emergence of the extreme right?*

Le Pen is not Poujade. This is not authentic fascism of the kind that results from a sudden convulsion of social power and from political failure. It springs from a resurgence of extremely strong values. But it is a watered-down form, deriving from a half-hearted sense of crisis, from an ebb, from an ill-defined reaction, from the 'saturation' of both left and right. Myth is absent. What you have is just naked virulence, violence exercised in the name of order and in response to the prevailing disorder.

PA *Could it be said that we are in what Emmanuel Mounier, the founder of the journal* Espirit, *described as the 'established disorder'?*

There is no revolutionary ambition any more. A certain continuity links Coluche, Montand and Le Pen – that of a civil protest against the inadequacy of the politicians. In cultural terms, the struggle for the Ecole Libre is part of the same phenomenon, though it does not coincide with it politically. Increasingly, people today fall back on smaller-scale goals, a tame concern for ecology and the movement against the State. This was already the case when the right was in power, though at that time hopes were still pinned on a form of rational socialism, one that has since failed dismally and definitively. In one sense, Le Pen has affinities with Reaganism. There are not two million Frenchmen of the extreme right; that number is swollen with the discontented. In addition, there are a lot of people who have acquired a taste for autonomy, for self-government at the local level, as exemplified by free choice of schools. The hypocrisy of Mitterrand makes me smile when, as a socialist with his back to the wall, he claims to want a lesser role for the State. Watching Le Pen on television against J. L. Servan-Schreiber, representative of a complacent upmarket liberalism, I wanted to smash his halo of self-satisfied conventional wisdom.

PA *I know many left-wingers who voted for Le Pen. How would you account for that?*

You are dealing there with local citizens, with remnants of a left-wing populism that respects a concentric structure of interests – I, my family, my tribe, my professional interests. It's a sentiment that Le Pen expresses admirably, and it's one that many communists still feel strongly. Faith in the welfare state has gone. This has to be admitted, but without undue praise for Le Pen. All the more so since a dialectical and pedagogic interpretative discourse remains the monopoly of the Left; the right has yet to reach the level of consciousness required to understand its own evolution.

PA *Is this to say that there is no longer a right wing?*

Politicians on both left and right collude to uphold the privileges of the political class. The march in favour of the Ecole Libre was bullshit in many respects, but the people were there; for despite being a moronic political manoeuvre it reflected real hopes. Regionalisation and decentralisation had been promised, but nothing had come of the promises. So the people occupied Paris to protest against their loss of local autonomy. That's very striking. Yves Montand on his own is nothing, merely an outgrowth of the intelligentsia, and not really subversive. But when the masses arrive on the scene we can't put up with him any more.

PA *Freedom, freedom, we have had three hundred years of the same political Manicheism. When the former defenders of liberty become its opponents, and its supposed enemies take to the streets in its name, does this not suggest that victory is changing sides?*

There is without a doubt a setback for the kind of liberties that socialism promotes, which accompanies the crude criticism of a State that is virtually totalitarian. But it is more subtle than this, more ambiguous; there is also a revival of a certain kind of libertarianism.

PA *On the American model? Reaganism has drawn heavily on this source.*

I'm not sure. What I know comes from American friends who, though anti-Reagan, acknowledge that he has sensed the exhaustion of the social energies on which socialism depended, being incapable of updating its own process of adaptation. Reagan grasped the importance of following the course of history, from Plato to Kennedy to MacNamara. His rough common sense works in his favour. He also respects, or certainly knows how to exploit, the kind of 'counter-powers' we have always had in France. What is really bad is that the Left's model of historical legitimacy, a 'moralised' Hegelianism, is now completely outmoded, even archaic. What we are witnessing is the revenge of ambiguity in political power, challenging the concept of politics itself.

PA *In short, a super-archaic dimension – traditional values, the family and so on – is screwing up the merely archaic. As Maurras said: this imbecilic nineteenth century.*

That's true. We see it happening in Poland, for example. Or with Jean-Paul II, the television Pope, who has succeeded in popularising some of the most appalling episcopal idiocies. If the term postmodernism means anything, it is based, paradoxically, on the nostalgia which is smashing up outdated modernism. It is an undertow, an ambiguous ebb-tide from the Stone Age.

PA *And yet modernity was invented by Baudelaire . . .*

Baudelaire thought of modernity as the 'hyper-modern' – that is, as the radical fluctuations of fashion. This is what Walter Benjamin said about him, when he described the price that modern man had to pay for his sensations, the collapse of personal experience, the shock of the new.

PA *Baudelaire paid a high price for his complicity in this collapse. And if I remember correctly, it was Benjamin who added that the 'laws of his poetry' shone in the sky of the Second Empire like a 'constellation without an atmosphere'. At the moment when the Fifth Republic embarks on a Bonapartist-style plebiscite, aren't we in what you call a* 'situation récurrentielle' *(literally a 'situation of recurrence')?*

No, a 'repetitive situation'. I can't detect any inevitability or predetermined fate: there is no trace of an impulse that does not originate in a personal deliberation. As for Baudelaire, he taught us to transpose the strategies of fashion. He invented dandyism, the immoral modernity that is the only true modernity. In this sense, the impulse from elsewhere reappears today in the form of the disappearance of modernity. Even the disappearance of the Communist Party is not an important event. It is an empty shell, like a car in the wreckers' yard. It is neither the coming of a new order, nor the shock wave of the disappearance of the aristocracy.

PA *In the* Communist Manifesto, *Marx said that the aristocracy would survive for centuries in literary polemics. I have the impression that it is making a comeback. What is to disappear next? The bourgeoisie? The working class?*

The working class has foundered in the quicksands. Perhaps it was never more than a metaphor of industrial society, a vestige. It has not managed to found a new symbolic order, and is now being swept away with the disappearance of production.

PA *Could artificial intelligence represent this new order?*

The computer represents a progressive technology, the highest point of a technology that is at once demented and backward-looking. It speculates on the information it accumulates. But there is no mental upheaval involved – everything fits, everything is stored, everything is literally programmed.

PA *What about the speed factor? The potential for virtually instantaneous operations, even if it does not actually restructure the intellectual field, seems to me to mark a decisive progress, inasmuch as all progress is first and foremost an acceleration.*

Why not? Computers work so quickly that there is no longer any movement – speed is aestheticised as technology. Yet this remains a new, 'implosive' form of technology, which entails the disappearance of all the others. Even within the McLuhanian circuit that heralded the return of tribal organisation, the computer has the vocation of 'tribalising'. The values it generates are exclusively tribal and domestic, and therefore modern. Suddenly, then, we can see paradoxical affinities between the super-archaic, exemplified by street action, and the super-technological, that the State struggles to monopolise for as long as possible. Progressively, the State loses out on all fronts, in the street and in modern technology.

PA *So a major break between the old and new seems to be on the way. But not as we expect it – only the unexpected occurs.*

Yes, but it doesn't reach the local level, and the result is tired and provincial. A culture like that of France which was based on universal values can only perish with the demise of universal values. France is disintegrating, but shamefully, in the midst of the worst kind of socialist hypocrisy, while even minor but unusual events are showing that right and left don't exist any more.

NOTES

Poujade, Pierre – Leader of a protest movement of small shopkeepers that, to everyone's surprise, obtained fifty deputies in the 1956 election. Jean-Marie Le Pen was among the Poujadist deputies before enlisting with the army in Algeria. The Poujadist movement as such disappeared in 1958, though a similar movement, with different leaders, (the CID-UNATI) emerged in the 1970s.

Le Pen, Jean-Marie – The charismatic leader of the *Front National*, a national-populist movement of the extreme right, in the anti-parliamentary and chauvinist tradition that developed in France between the wars with the Croix de Feu. Former Poujadist deputy Le Pen enlisted as a parachutist officer in Algeria and has been accused of carrying out torture there: he has brought several successful legal actions against those who make these accusations; facts concerning the Algerian war being covered by an amnesty, his accusers have not been able to use the evidence that could substantiate their claims. With his oratorical gifts and the use of slogans such as 'Frenchmen First', Le Pen has brought the extreme right back into mainstream politics, exploiting the popular discontent born of the crisis and fears of unemployment and linking it with a chauvinism that borders on overt racism.

Esprit – A journal founded by Emmanuel Mounier and situated in the tradition of Social Catholicism that appeared in France at the start of the century around the journal *Le Sillon* (of Marc Sangnier). This essentially intellectual current was revitalised by involvement in the Resistance; its significance is to be interpreted against the background of the disappearance of a Christian Democrat political force that the MRP had represented from 1945 to 1958.

Coluche and **Montand** – The remarkable career of Ronald Reagan, from 'B' movie actor to President of the United States, has inspired two French show business personalities with a taste for politics. Coluche (Michel Colucci) made a reputation with savage send-ups of commonplace stupidity and popular racism. Of anarchist tendencies, his decision in December 1980 to stand for the Presidency of the Republic was a gesture of contempt for politics and politicians at the time when Giscard d'Estaing's re-election looked certain. Intellectuals immediately acclaimed his candidature. He was the object of threats from the extreme right, that accused him of slighting the 'honour of the police' by playing the lead role in a film entitled 'Inspecteur la Bavure'; the film's innocuous plot scarcely warranted such an outcry, though since it was not yet generally released the content had merely been inferred from the title. A dazzling but somewhat pusillanimous character, Coluche dropped his candidature and the election campaign recovered a more serious aspect, culminating in the election of Mitterrand. The itinerary of singer and actor Yves Montand is similar in some respects. Formerly a fellow traveller of the Parti Communiste, he developed a violent antipathy towards his former comrades following the Soviet intervention in Czechoslovakia in 1968. Invited to appear in political programmes on television, Montand appeared to believe that he had a national vocation on the lines of Reagan's example; but this episode ended pathetically when it became known that he had asked for a large fee to appear on a programme in which the political figures invited are not paid.

Ecole Libre – The question of secularism in schools has dogged French political life since the nineteenth century; Church and State have battled for the monopoly in education, opposing the rights of parents and freedom of conscience to the right of all children to receive a civic instruction. Under the Fourth Republic, the Catholic schools ('*école libre*') finally obtained financial subsidies equal to those received by State schools (the so-called contract of 'association'). Plans by the Mauroy government to make staff of the private schools state employees were interpreted as a threat to the '*école libre*' and gave rise to mass demonstrations that provoked the fall of the government.

Regionalisation and decentralisation – France has traditionally been administered on the Napoleonic model of a central power represented in the departments by the Paris-based authority's agent: the Prefect. For the first Mauroy government (1981–2), decentralisation involved transferring some of the powers of the Prefects (renamed Commissioners of the Republic) to the elected departmental bodies (*Conseils Généraux*). Regionalisation, an older initiative, involved creating groups of departments (the régions) with their own elected bodies (the *Conseils Régionnaux*) and regional Prefects (or IGAMEs).

Maurras – A representative figure of the nationalist and elitist extreme right, close to monarchist circles, and whose organ *Action francaise* was influential chiefly between 1900 and 1939.

Plebiscite – A political procedure of the Second Empire whereby the electorate was called to pronounce upon the action of the Emperor. The referendums of the Fifth Republic were plebiscitary in that De Gaulle made his resignation depend on the result – he called, in his words, for a 'clear and massive yes'. Moreover, De Gaulle's referendums often involved giving a single answer to several questions.

Parti Communiste – Representing more than a quarter of the votes at the Liberation, its share of the poll never dropped below one-fifth before 1978. A dramatic loss of support since then (down now to roughly one-tenth) is due in part to the inept leadership of Georges Marchais, but also to the more general phenomenon described as the 'end of ideology'. Rhetorical hyperbole notwithstanding, it remains an exaggeration to speak of its 'disappearance' – its strength is merely comparable to that of the *Front National.*

6 A Time of Promiscuity

Interview with John Strand (JS)

JS *In 'Transaesthetics'*[1] *you use a lot of medical metaphors to describe value. You refer to the 'epidemic' of value, to 'metastasis' and to 'cancer'. Does this mean that value as such no longer exists?*

Obviously there is no more value once value has become an epidemic. For value to have any meaning there has to be a substantial reference point, and to make a value judgement we need some kind of distance, some sort of staging so that something with value stands apart. One has to be able to make an evaluation. If these things existed then there would no longer be an epidemic. But we live in a time of promiscuity, of total contiguity.

Value is like a chain reaction, an infinitely extensible web. I think the word 'epidemic' is applicable as well to the economic sphere, which involves the most immediate and superficial kind of value. Here, too, there is a close parallel with value in art or value in general, in the way that speculation – the extraordinary extension and expansion of value – has transformed and brought traditional capitalism to an end. But the same is true in Eastern Europe, where ideologies have lost their meaning or value. That's how the novelist Aleksandr Zinoviev describes communism – it has long since ceased to represent a system of values, an accepted hierarchy of social values.

Both capitalism and communism are coming to an end due to a consensus that is in fact quite comparable and which I think is like a total epidemic, or if you like a total investment. Everything is invested, everything is valuable and no one recognises any value. Democratic values have become so universal, so accepted and recognised that virtually no one disbelieves in them. Since value is universally shared, it is the same everywhere, therefore no value exists.

JS *Neo-Geo artists in the United States have quoted you a great deal. Have you had any contact with them?*

Not much. I went to New York in 1987 to give a lecture. It was really mad – every seat was sold out in advance, and I knew nothing about it. I had met Peter Halley in Paris but that was all I knew of him until I arrived there and I saw them all, but I've never had any close ties with any of them. Moreover, I didn't really want to get involved with them because I was asked for all sorts of things – prefaces, an endorsement, alibi-type texts – and I didn't want to be used as an alibi! It all developed outside my control and that's better for sure.

There was a rather serious misunderstanding about the word 'simulacrum'. It was used like a leitmotif and a slogan but not at all as an idea. My touchstone was Andy Warhol. I had to address his work because at bottom he seemed to be the origin of the simulation, and everything after him seemed to me to be overproduction. One no longer knows what the real consequences of his art are and what is just publicity.

Personally, I don't dislike or have a negative judgement of Neo-Geo artists. Of course it is pointless to ask whether there is anything original there. Even in simulation there is an original process at work and a process that is not original. For me, simulation is not an original process, but then those artists can say to me, 'We've gone further in simulation than you', and why not? They're right. They simulate simulation. It makes your head spin!

JS *You have also written that art is disappearing, that everything is becoming aesthetic.*

When people tell me, 'What you say about art being finished, about art having disappeared, is totally absurd', it's true that I've said things like that, but it's not well expressed because I don't mean that art has disappeared all of a sudden. Other people tell me: 'You write about the end of history.' That's silly: there is history, there is always history. It is the whole complicated process of enfranchisement, of reaching saturation point, of the scattering and regrouping of history. I don't mean the end in the stupid sense of the word. People simplify your thoughts and pigeonhole you and then they refute you. That's tough because it's impossible to reconstruct your argument. You can't correct things afterwards.

In America I have an exorbitant and false image. It's hard to fight against that. If other people accuse me of being postmodern, I say 'I'm not postmodern', but everyone tells me I am and I can't do anything about it.

JS *You also refer to the profound indifference associated with art for art's sake.*

If art is the criterion for art, then value is relative. But the artist makes a big investment and it's true that this art has meaning practically only for the artist. Strangely enough, in this era of communication, dialogue and mass involvement, each performance refers completely to each one of us because no one has the time any longer to look, judge and discuss. What has happened is only meaningful for actors at the very moment when something happens.

Instead of things taking on an ever vaster meaning, on the contrary I believe that meaning is shrinking. What is for certain, what cannot be ignored, is the fact that each artist is doing his own thing, and even though it is objectively worthless it has to be referred to as art, as a game. Beyond that soap bubble lies indifference.

Differences do exist, exchanges are made, a system exists that is made up more and more of the totally exceptional and the universally indifferent. A break in the equilibrium between subject and object, interior and exterior, is quite palpable, to my mind.

JS *You have said that value rises quickly when judgement is not exercised to stabilise it. Is this the explanation for some of the phenomenal prices paid for Picassos recently?*

It's inconceivable, isn't it? In fact there is no more imagination. It's a fact, but it has no meaning. In the imagination of an artist or of culture in general it's quite a different matter. It's a form of speculation, and yet speculation is missing in that the individual doesn't really control things. No one even makes a 'profit': the profit isn't even the object any longer. It's dizzying, it's very, very contagious and it's fascinating. It captivates everyone. Even if one reacts morally and says, 'This is disgusting and scandalous', in reality everyone is fascinated.

NOTE

1. J. Baudrillard (1993), *The Transparency of Evil: Essays on Extreme Phenomena*, London: Verso, pp. 14–19. [Editors]

7 Forgetting Critiques

Interview with Dianne Hunter (DH)

DH *To what field do you regard your work as belonging? What form did your intellectual development take?*

I started out writing literature. I was interested particularly in poetry. I didn't start writing theory until I was 36 or 38 years old. Lately there has been a rupture in the style of my writing; I have broken with theory and began writing literature again, as in *Cool Memories* [1987], an account of my trip to America, a notebook of five years of my life, 1980 to 1985. The rhythm and style of that book breaks with my theoretical works.

By training I was a Germanist. I did studies in German philosophy, the history of philosophy and the history of ideas as a young man; and that philosophical education, above all influenced by my study of Nietzsche, remains as a philosophical drive in my work.

Poetically, I was much impressed by Artaud, Rimbaud and Bataille.

Psychoanalysis interests me, but not the academic discipline called psychology. I don't think I belong to any particular field. My work is outside the disciplines, or transdisciplinary. When I was appointed to teach at Nanterre, I was appointed as a sociologist, but that was in a very free era. I think my work has a transversality, a cross-disciplinarity. I am a metaphysician and a moralist. I write manifestos.

DH *What were the important elements in the intellectual context of your training that influenced your development as a writer?*

Before 1968, I was much influenced by the 1960s Situationists, who were radical internationalists, anarchists, leftists. I was distantly Marxist, anti-media, and against the advertisement establishment. I was taken with the ideas of Marcuse.

Then, after 1968, after the Algerian war, a theoretical constellation came together for me, so I began writing theory. I wanted to transform radical politics into radical theory. Nineteen sixty-eight was a riverbank marking the end of a development that had lasted more than thirty years.

DH *Who are the other writers who have most influenced your work? Do you have any masters?*

Nietzsche, Artaud, Bataille. I read Faulkner when I was in my twenties. I was attracted by his universe, its metaphysics of abstraction, his fabulation, and his way of reading reality. More recently, in my political period, I was influenced by Sartre, Barthes especially, Benjamin, Bataille and Borges, and of course Marx and Freud. Among my contemporaries, Derrida and Lyotard are friends, but I don't read them. If I have a master, it is Nietzsche.

DH *In the United States, you are often cited as a defender of seduction. How would you explain your concept of seduction?*

My first books criticised the idea of production and Marxist dialectics, which I associate with death. Production is about material, value, the market and the law; seduction is about play, the rules of the game of appearances. I am interested in a strategy which differs from the materialist emphasis on production. I prefer a strategy that slides to one that confronts.

Another game was sexual liberation. So I wanted to write a critique of the theory of desire and of the sexual liberation movement. I critiqued the imperative of the liberation movement in place of critiquing desire, which would have been too frontal an opposition. Therefore, I passed over to the theme of seduction.

I am interested in the play in the rules which are not transposable to politics or to production. I want to change the rules of what is considered 'reality'. Part of reality is play and the phenomenology of seduction. I am interested in the metaphysics of seduction, in what appears and disappears, not in the ordinary sense of the word seduction.

Seduction for me is the turning aside of the world, the turning aside of reality, a challenge and a duel with the world, with the law of the world, with the reality principle.

Art participates in seduction, in the power of illusion. This is something different from the mass media's fascinations and manipulations. Seduction in the mass media is not a seduction in the strong sense of seduction. Advertisements practise a vulgar seduction – and that is a degradation of the term seduction. I prefer to use the concept of seduction in a strong sense – as it relates to the field of dreams. This sense is outside the idea of seduction of the senses.

My concept of seduction is a critique of production, but not a rational critique. I preferred to pass on to the idea of the enchanted moment. I regard seduction as the fatal strategy – playing with death. My notion of seduction is a fatal notion. There is a fatality in it that has to do with predestination of signs and loss of identity.

I saw this as a problematic of symbolic exchange and death.

This caused cuts and ruptures in my theoretical persona, and I thus adopted a different strategy of fatality – aphorisms of a fragmented self. This is the style of *Amérique* [1986], which is marked by a disappearance of theory. In that book, writing itself becomes the fatal strategy. There is a materialisation of seduction as a fatal strategy in the writing.

DH *Why do you regard America as an obscene desert?*

I love the desert, its emptiness, its total indifference. It is neither nature nor culture. It is obscene in the sense that it does not have a scene. It has no play, no seduction. America is radically obscene; there everything is on show. This radicalisation of the obscene is an extreme increase in force. There is nothing hidden. All is visible, illuminated. My description of America is enthusiastic. The desert is a metaphor. My response to it is visceral.

DH *How do you see the relation between your valorisation of appearances and the critique of the look and of representation offered in recent French philosophy, by Derrida for example?*

The deconstructive critique of the 1960s and 1970s is a critical field with subtle conclusions. I don't work with that critique. I am interested in what is beyond representation, in the field of the appearances and disappearances of things. I think things are already deconstructed. I have been interested in starting something new, forgetting critiques. Simulation is an extreme of representation; it is beyond appearances. Simulation is not the same as appearances; it belongs to the order of playing. Simulation is a work of mobilisation of signs. My interest in simulation has no direct relation with Derrida. Barthes influenced me, especially his ideas on marginality. My work is outside of deconstruction. For me, the fatal is the same sign as appearance and disappearance.

I am interested in the rules of the game of the symbolic. By 'symbolic'

I do not mean the Lacanian symbolic, but the universe of mental simulation.

Lacan's idea of the sign as a chain of signifiers chains up seduction. For me, the symbolic order is the register of desire, where ideology is fatal. The Lacanian sign is a chain of representations, but I am interested in another kind of sign, which is elliptical, as in poetry, where the sign is fatal. Poetry is a seductive duel. This is anti-semiotic analysis. Semiology was interesting in 1968, but twenty years is enough. It is time to go beyond the study of representation and semiology.

DH *How do you introduce the question of sexual difference into your theory of seduction? Does the question of sexual difference have a pertinence for you? What place does a reflection on power have for you here?*

I am interested in the power of seduction. I study the power of fascination and incarnation. I read Foucault before I wrote *De La Séduction* [1979]. Foucault's notion of power interested me. According to his analysis, power is being exerted everywhere. I decided to reverse this and say that power does not exist. My hypothesis is that masculinity does not exist; it is a gigantic story of simulation. My idea is that power is on the side of the feminine and of simulation. Liberation movements stay on the side of an exacerbation of sexual difference. There is difference when there is power. In seduction there is a provocation and a duel. In the game, there is neither equality nor difference: sexual difference is secondary. In the game, there is contamination, a loss of differences. Indeterminacy, a lack of difference, is an unhappy result of sexual liberation. I am interested in seduction apart from ideology. Seduction *plays* with sexual difference. It *plays* with desire. It plays with sexual difference, but it does not believe in it. Seduction does not make desire and sexual difference an issue except to reverse or play with it. Seduction dissolves sexual difference. It creates a scene. The power of desire is what is played with in this scene. It is a game where one plays with the power of desire, and the power of desire is in play. This is a rule of the game in the symbolic. We must distinguish between virtual power and positive power. Positive power is mastery of the real world. Seduction is mastery of the symbolic world.

DH *What does the idea of symbolic exchange mean for you?*

I have passed beyond that theme. When I was interested in anthropology and production, symbolic exchange had to do with semiotic spiralling. It was connected to my reading of Mauss and the study of primitive societies. Now that idea is too nostalgic for me.

DH *In 1968, you were calling for a taking of the floor to speak as part of taking power. Mark Poster has pointed out that your celebration of* la parole *implies a total presence in the subject who speaks.*[1] *Is the divided subject an issue in your work?*

In 1968, *prendre la parole* was to act against those who controlled power; the word opposed the code that imposed subjectivity. I wanted a radical subjectivity to articulate itself. Now that is all passé. Desire, the subject, and *la parole* are on one side; and on the other is the object. I am interested in what happens in the world of objects. As far as I am concerned, the subject of the subject is past. I am interested in the object, which is silent, a seductive desert. It is the object and seduction which attract me in place of the subject and desire.

NOTE

1. J. Baudrillard (1975), *The Mirror of Production*, St Louis: Telos, p. 11.

8 Cover Story

Interview with Serge Bramly (SB)

SB *You take photos, and, as if that weren't enough, you've begun to exhibit them. How did you get to the other side of the mirror?*

First of all, it's not a qualitative leap. Photography slipped in surreptitiously, there wasn't any revelation. Up until the eighties I didn't have a very high opinion of photography. I felt a slight sense of disdain, but that was in the air. The whole thing actually started through something like a contagion . . . I was given a little camera in Japan and I began by photographing Siberia from above, on the return flight.

SB *You don't see it as a compromise?*

No, and above all not with aesthetics. For me it was like a collage. I was interested by a certain form of the appearance of objects. I don't pretend to have any subjective, aesthetic vision of the world, nor any kind of interpretation, nor any style . . . I'm not aiming for a photography that would compose another universe. No, I photograph what appears to me, moment by moment. You crystallise on an object, or rather a given object makes itself seen. And the photographic subject stays quite close to degree zero.

SB *You have written that it is always the object which demands to be photographed, that we have only a bit part in its staging. But even if the role of the photographer, of the subject, is dramatically reduced, something of it still remains.*

You can't cut out all the aesthetic references. A visual culture comes through in the framing, in the light you choose. I don't deny I have an aesthetic subconscious like everyone else. But I remain very suspicious, very refractory towards aesthetic transcendence. In my writing and in my photos I try to eliminate even the smallest explicit reference to Art with a capital A.

SB *Why this rejection? To say art is dead seems a bit simple.*

I don't want to put a value judgement on what's happening right now, but for me let's just say there isn't much sense to it. We live in a generalised aestheticism. Any aspect of banality can make its claim to be aesthetic, as Warhol proved. Art still pretends to be art, while it is really no more than a kind of metalanguage of banality . . . So beyond that, what remains is the appearance and disappearance of the raw object, in a kind of obviousness. It is what it is and you have to try to take it just like that, to short-circuit the intervention of the subject, to disappear for the appearance of the object.

SB *But even that is already a theory.*

As a matter of fact, the practice of photography brings me much more immediate pleasures . . . [*laughter*].

SB *Of what sort?*

The plunge into a world of surfaces, of the obvious. The obvious is not just beautiful in the artistic sense of the word; it's fascinating. I'm fascinated by the object that appears, that wants to appear. By object, I mean some matter, some light, a situation, a landscape, a silhouette perhaps, but not a face, no resemblance, no meaning or psychology. I must capture this object at the moment of its appearance, before it takes on a meaning. And the lens constitutes a fantastic instrument for that, because it cuts you off from the world and puts you in direct transition with the object . . . To get back to pleasure, for me photography is also linked to the idea of travelling, to the flux of the city, to the desert, even if some of my pictures have been taken in immediate, intimate surroundings . . . In the end, travel is the source.

SB *Mediumistic voyages . . .*

Something like that. Making something emerge from elsewhere, from alongside reality. It's more intense than the situation of writing, which implies mastery. To photograph is not to be master of things – on the contrary.

SB *But there is this idea of going beyond aesthetics.*

It's better to go beyond. It would be annoying to go behind, to have to return to some pre-aesthetic state. But on the other hand, you do get back to the fetish nonetheless. Roger Caillois wrote very perceptively about that, in a text on Picasso. He says that tomorrow's artists will no longer be artists. They will no longer create works; they will fabricate objects of an almost anthropological nature, just as Warhol, the precursor, fabricates images that come close to fetishistic ritual, that are far in any case from aesthetics. The fetish object (etymologically, the artefact) has to do with extreme illusion, with the power of illusion and ritual. That's why it can concern almost anything, because it isn't a matter of quality. It's a matter of power.

SB *So we would return to a kind of primitivism?*

No. At present, the aesthetic dimension is coming apart all on its own; art is no longer able to transfigure itself, no longer able to attain the status of illusion in the strong sense of the word. In general, it's very flat, a low-intensity sort of slap-dash bricolage – whereas the fetish is the object of a very intense bricolage. According to Freud, fetishism attaches to the last objects glimpsed before the plunge into sexuality. Thus these objects possess all the energy of that which is about to disappear. Nothing predestined them for such a role. Only their proximity to the appearance/disappearance of the genitals gives them their ephemeral force. It's an intense, ephemeral ritual. It's not exactly the rite of a subject: in fetishism, there is no more subject or object.

SB *That's what makes it interesting?*

Yes. The subject is lost, the object imposes itself, inverting the normal order of things. The result is something which is neither subject nor object, and thus is situated beyond the configuration of aesthetics, where there is a correlation of subject and object, a relative mastery of one by the other, and so on. It's another kind of dramaturgy.

SB *You say the same things about art as about politics, economics or other aspects of culture.*

We're witnessing a generalised passage over the limits. Things function beyond their proper end, they don't make any more sense and yet they still work, sometimes even better than before, but as extreme phenomena. Whether they are extremely positive or extremely negative, the results are always perverse. In politics, for example, you have a transfusion of all ideologies, and therefore radical indifference.

SB *Degenerating into what?*

It can take on the aspect of previous convulsions, of fascism for example – but pre-war fascism was ideologically messianic, it wasn't made of indifference, but on the contrary, of a passion. Today's indifference is creating implosive phenomena whose process is completely unknown. And if there is a rational therapy for collective passions, there is no therapy for indifference. The hypotension of the political system is incurable . . .

SB *In your latest book,* L'illusion de la fin ou la grève des événements [The Illusion of the End or Events on Strike], *you talked about creating an anonymous, clandestine disinformation agency, which could be indifferently baptised Transfatal Express, International Epidemic, and so on. Are irony and derision the final weapons of thought?*

Things can no longer be grasped rationally. In that case, what can you do but virally inject a kind of violent reversibility into the world? Pataphysics[1] is a kind of acid. And Jarry was exactly that, denouncing reality as 'ubuesque', as an inflatable structure, and existence as a hyperbolic pretension. This superstition of existence is completely ridiculous. All these inflatable structures must be deflated, whence this fatal irony.

SB *It's a rather elitist kind of remedy.*

I'm not sure the pretension to existence is vulgar. Of course, everyone will always claim they exist. And if you contest that, they respond that you're crazy. At another level, though, there exists a kind of fundamental incredulity, even towards one's own existence. If you awaken this incredulity, you can touch off some extraordinary things . . .

SB *The denial of existence could then be the super-illusion that allows one to go on, despite everything . . .*

Yes, there is a strategy of the illusion. To rediscover not existence, in which we believe so little, but instead the vital illusion – that would be the greatest game. We lose track of it in this breakneck realisation of everything, which leads to extreme indifference. Fatal and ironic: those are the two qualities which are no longer at play in rationalised existence. There is no more destiny, and no more illusion. It's a mortifying situation. But if you contest it, people think they're defending their lives by rejecting you as a bearer of bad news. They confuse the message and its bearer. If you say the war did not take place, as I did at the time of the Gulf War, it's much worse than the news of the war itself.

SB *In a televised report about Bosnia, I heard a woman say that she thought ceaselessly about your books, about* La transparence du mal [The Transparency of Evil], *and wished that you would come to confirm what's happening in her country.*

I don't know what she meant by that. The problem is not to go and verify the ideas in a book . . . As for confirming pain and distress, anyone can do that. It must have been the idea of 'speaking' this distress, this evil whose cause is unknown. One suffers, one submits, without seeing the finality of it all; there comes a total confusion where no one can get their bearings any more. Victims, torturers, it's the circulation of evil and its way of transpiring even through the appearances of good; there's no chance to make any more sense of it . . . You can die for a cause, but as someone said, I don't remember who, there is no cause worth dying for today. That's certainly the phrase which best testifies to the total powerlessness of our epoch.

SB *That doesn't keep people from killing each other more or less everywhere . . .*

And lightheartedly – but it's only an effect, a perverse effect. Massacres, purifications, yes, but without any historical finality. It's a recycling of waste products. And that's where the real distress lies. There is no distinction today between good and evil; even humanitarianism can't find its meaning, it works as a substitute ideology . . . Because we haven't gone beyond good and evil. We haven't gone beyond humanity; we are still short of the human and the inhuman, in a magma of events. Things are so interconnected that there are always more and more events, with fewer and fewer consequences. And the media only accelerate the indifference, the over-information, the depression through excess, the asphyxia. Even our moral consciousness is overfed. But you can't escape miraculously, through some vitalising regression. No, you have to enter the system. You have to become viral yourself, assume your virality.

Personally, all I have is writing. Writing itself can become fractal, or in any case renounce all artificial composition, eliminating references, causes and effects, origin and finality. That results in a somewhat disconnected writing, one which troubles and disconcerts as well, not only because its content seems to be pessimistic – which is not true – but because it has an ironic form, a form of relinquishment and challenge. It's a virulent writing that forces people to secrete antibodies. Because it has no need to analyse everything, it puts an end to this state of things where nothing ends. Through writing, you can put an end to something, bring it to disappearance, and this disappearance has an immediate viral effect. Writing also goes directly to the way things appear and disappear. It's never constructive or reconstructive. It installs a deadly reversibility.

SB *Isn't it contradictory for a philosopher to lay his hopes on writing?*

First of all, I make no claim to the title of philosopher. The history of ideas doesn't interest me; it's had no determining influence on me. I may have written a few conventional analyses . . . But then it turned into something else. The state of things came to an extreme, and the writing had to radicalise itself as well. It has its own logic, and by a somewhat mad autonomisation it begins to go on independently at a certain point, drawing you beyond what you believed you were doing. Those are the good moments. The theory pierces the object. There is no more real object, the two bend to the same form, and a resonance is established, a consonance of words and things – fortunately, otherwise it would be pure madness . . .

SB *Could artists also adopt this technique?*

I don't know. Personally, I'm no longer involved in political analysis, nor in philosophy, nor in sociology . . . Whereas the artists, as I see them, are still fascinated by art. They don't leave behind the exercise of art, they're still within a history, a will to create, to communicate. No doubt there are some who get out of it. At least through their singularity. They do things which are no longer exactly art, but acts, types of acting out that let them escape the perpetual reference to art. I'm thinking of Bacon, maybe because there is a superhuman side to him, something which imposes itself with such force, and which at the same time has lost its relays, which participates in another universe. That's true of Hopper as well.

SB *In* The Transparency of Evil, *you said that the art market followed aesthetic inflation, that there was no more ceiling for prices because no one can judge the value of the works. Would you write this chapter differently now that prices have tumbled?*

No. And I don't believe in this re-establishment of the market that everyone is talking about; that would be too easy. The art market, like the stock market, is a domain where speculation can have free rein, because the artwork permits a high degree of fetishisation. Negative fetishisation in this case, because the concept of artwork survives in aesthetic surplus-value. It's a mystery to me that it can continue, that we can have on one hand such a banalised aestheticisation of everything, and on the other, the sudden crystallisation of a priceless object . . . That could be considered a good thing in so far as it's an excess, but you can hardly assimilate it to Bataille's critical excess, to the unheard-of prodigality of potlatch. It's interesting, though, in the sense that the system is animated by the perverse temptation to go beyond its own limits. In itself, that's also an extreme phenomenon.

SB *I have the impression that, according to you, we've come to some sort of total entropy and are reduced to waiting, perhaps in vain, for a big bang.*

I don't know whether there still exists an art of living under these conditions. One could, at best, be a stoic. In its way, stoicism forms a nice strategy of indifference. The stoic is seen as moral, virtuous; but this radicalist vision is quite immoral, at bottom. In such indifference there is a defiance that goes beyond the ordinary indifference of the world. In our culture, until the eighteenth century, things were conceived of in terms of pleasure. Then the idea of pleasure disappeared and in its place you found, much more democratically, much more anchored in modernity, the idea of desire. Then everything was desire, object of desire. It was the universal justification and, along with enjoyment [*jouissance*], it formed a new way of thinking, of living . . . But desire has disappeared in turn. What do we have now? A strange, rather extenuated thing, which I call rights. It's no longer a question of really existing, but of having the right to existence. There is, in my mind, no more depressive mode. Pleasure was an illusion, but people could manage it as an illusion. Desire was more real; it was an attenuated form of illusion, but in the end it was always desire for a (more or less lost) object, there was still a rapport to the phantasmatic dimension, to carnality. In the era of rights, on the contrary, it's enough to legalise one's existence, to establish one's identity, and so on. The reality show, for example, is the ultra-democratised form of access to the surface, to existence. It's not an extremely glorious status. All the fuses have blown and life's only intensity is juridical. Since a thing is possible, it must be demanded, even if no one really wants it; there's no question of renouncing as soon as another has obtained it. It's as though the individual had been virtualised in the possibilities opened up by the system.

SB *If I follow you, that means we get artists whose works have no other end than to prove they are artists.*

Yes, whereas if art tried to bring illusion back into question, to invent other rules of the game, it could pierce through . . . I think there are breaches, sanctuaries, I'm not in despair at all. But I'm torn between the idea that you have to completely go with the system, as far as possible, playing its perverse game, and at the same time the idea that what's needed is not to be on the defensive, but to already be in search of means that would allow you to play your cards even after the loss of immunity . . . in a world of radical illusion where you no longer have the right to anything, where even life is not a right. Only survival is a right.

SB *What do you think of when you speak of breaches or sanctuaries?*

There are points where the system breaks down. I don't mean that one must infiltrate these breaches, but by going along with the system, even faster than it, you can turn it inside out. Let's take the recent events in the East. They haven't proved constructive, they haven't created new zones of freedom. Suddenly a political bloc fell apart. You could almost talk in terms of plate tectonics: a big black hole formed. These are events in the logic of Jarry: the history of an aimless floating towards emptiness instead of a concentration at the centre, as though the ensemble had reached its limits and suddenly lost all immunity. People call me a nihilist, but it's the events that are nihilistic. And there you have to make a wager, and convince yourself that being sucked in by the void could function as a kind of antigravity.

SB *So everyone at their own level could use new breakdowns to provoke kinds of clashes . . .*

Yes, create by making emptiness. Art is not a transhistorical phenomenon. It has a history and therefore can have a symbolic death. Things were much more exalting at the beginning of this century, when people like Benjamin could simultaneously possess previous culture in its entirety and foresee the collapse that was coming. But today artists perpetuate a collapse which no longer has the value of a revelation. You have nothing more than effects which lose themselves in nature, like waste products. It's somewhat like material production: there are more waste products than consumer goods. And while the real products are used up, consumed, which is what makes them useful, the waste products are eternal, unrecyclable, non-degradable . . . So it's in vain that art has been desacralised for a century now: it can't be said that this desacralisation of art has constituted a veritable event.

SB *Art has been desacralised, but artists have been made sacred.*

Yes, and they've limited themselves to managing the catastrophe, which can't be expected to become an event either, since it is interminable. The death of art is endlessly diluted. I have the impression of a great dilution, like in Benveniste's theory about the memory of water: there isn't a single molecule left, yet the effect remains the same in the total absence of substance. The principle of art, its energy, the power of illusion, can all completely disappear, but we continue living in aesthetics as though it was immortal. People thought: when everything has been banalised, when art has been purged of all its ideological superstructures, superstitions and so on, then we'll touch its very reality, the pure artistic act – but in fact we've fallen back on the same consecration. It's like an integrated circuit, entirely closed off; like politics, it is in a certain sense indestructible.

Translated by Brian Holmes

NOTE

1. The turn of the century satirist Alfred Jarry, creator of the nonsensical character Ubu, defined pataphysics as 'the science of imaginary solutions, symbolically according the lineaments with the properties of virtual objects'.

9 Symbolic Exchange: Taking Theory Seriously

Interview with Roy Boyne (RB) and Scott Lash (SL)

SL *What struck me when I read Mike Gane's Introduction to the English translation of* Symbolic Exchange and Death[1] *was something you said in an interview of 1991 about this being a more serious, conceptual, philosophical book than many of the others you have written. You were a little disappointed at its being picked up by the fine arts milieu and not much discussed from the analytical, conceptual point of view.*

That's right. It didn't produce much of an echo or resonance. But, where the fine arts people are concerned, they have mainly latched on to the simulation, simulacra side of my work, rather than *Symbolic Exchange.* They took their lead much more from the simulacra-simulations-seduction line of thinking.

It's true that the book was well received, but not discussed. That's part of a more general problem. I'm not received as a philosopher's philosopher. I'm not institutionally legitimated, so to speak, by the philosophers – and not just by the academic, professional philosophers, but also by the rather more subtle philosophers, if I may put it that way: those people I consider to be the true philosophers. Even among them, the book wasn't discussed. I regretted that a little, but in the end I took the view that that was the rule of the game, or, rather, the law of that milieu.

In a way, the barrier erected against me in that world has grown bigger. Some of my other books on what might be termed more frivolous subjects (not for me, but that's how they see it) have been taken as a pretext not to confront the philosophical problematic I've been concerned with – the question of the object, of reversibility, and so on.

SL *This book is published in a serious collection read by theoretical sociologists, cultural theorists and philosophers . . .*

That may change the way things work out.

SL *Our PhD students read Baudrillard, Bataille, Levinas, Heidegger . . . all together.*

Yes, I'm a great admirer of the way these things are done in other countries. In France, barriers are put up, people have their territories. Elsewhere – in Australia, Brazil, Britain, the USA – things are quite different. People read everything at the same time, which is good in a way. At least there are cross-fertilisations which don't happen in France on account of a sort of marginalisation mechanism there, which is also a form of sclerosis of the intellectual milieu. But that's how it is. Obviously, I haven't been accepted by the sociologists. But I haven't been adopted by the philosophers either [*laughter*]. I've been rejected by both the feminists and the political activists, so in the end there isn't much left. A situation of total freedom.

RB *The question which interests me is that of subjectivity. How do things stand now with subjectivity? What is the relationship between subjectivity and postmodernity, subjectivity and symbolic exchange? Kantian morality, for example, is built on the terrain of decision, judgement . . .*

My reply here perhaps justifies the barrier philosophers have put up against me to some extent, in that my thinking isn't grounded in a study of the history of ideas, of Kant, and so on. I decided rather on a kind of 'take-off' without references, creating an almost artificial situation, a kind of radical phenomenology . . .

The problem which obsessed me – I had a personal obsession from the outset – was that of the object, the material object, the object of consumption and so on, and that subsequently became a kind of problematic of the object in a much more metaphysical sense, or even a sense which goes beyond that. Though this doesn't apply to my first books, from *Symbolic Exchange* onwards there was an attempt to look beyond the strategies of the subject, beyond subjectivity, beyond the subject of knowledge, of history, of power and so on, and to go and take a look at the object side – which in sociological terms also meant looking at the masses, and so on. Or in the sciences, to look at the object, not the subject of science. So, the kind of fascination or seduction came from the object.

This wasn't so much a philosophical argument. There was, rather, a seduction, a temptation to find a kind of dual relation with the object, which wouldn't be a subject–object or dialectical relation, to see if there wasn't perhaps on the object side (though you can't go over totally to the object side, of course, since that inevitably involves a paradox, even an impasse), to see whether there wasn't another logic developing, or another paralogic, another strategy, whether from the political, sociological and also philosophical point of view – or even from a scientific one. Obviously, I'm not an expert in the sciences, but I know that the problem of the object in the sciences is a crucial one today. So, in my first books, and up to *Symbolic Exchange*, while I drew on the official disciplines – semiology, psychoanalysis, Marxism – I always tried to come at those disciplines from the angle of their object, to take the side of the object against the discipline that claimed to be master of it. That was more or less what I was doing there.

Now, admittedly, this isn't a particularly philosophical approach. It's really more pataphysical, though let's not get too bogged down in that term here. But there was also a kind of Situationism in this – taking the world as it is, taking it as a kind of radical self-evidence. And rediscovering radicality not in radical subjectivity, but in radical objectivity – though not in an objectivity of a rationalist type, obviously. But there was a kind of *parti pris*, a kind of gamble or challenge there; so this wasn't a serene, objective philosophical choice, but, quite the contrary, a kind of *parti pris* to choose the object. And also a decision to try to seduce the object. The problem was no longer one of producing the object, producing the methods for investigating the object, but seducing the object [*laughter*] – being seduced by it and seducing it. This is a quite other type of relation.

RB *Is there any connection with concepts like Melanie Klein's part object?*

There are aspects of that. Speaking of the object is too general. It can take on all kinds of forms: fractal, partial, and can even be perfectly enigmatic, the object having the form of a puzzle, a paradox – something unintelligible in some way. And the objective of theory here – let's call it theory, because it isn't philosophy we're talking about – is, ultimately, to make the world more unintelligible. Not to explain the world and cast light on it. We aren't in the Enlightenment any more. The object of theory can possibly be conceived in terms of symbolic exchange, where the law is that something is given to you and you have to give it back and, if possible, give back *more* – the *surplus-value* of symbolic exchange. The position is, then, that the world is given to us, and given to us as unintelligible; we have to render it even more unintelligible. We have to render it, to give it back [*le rendre*]; we don't necessarily have to master it, calculate it, compute it, but we have to give it back more enigmatic than it is. This is the problem as I see it now. The world is, in a way, too intelligible, too transparent. Though perhaps not truly so, at bottom. But we live in a system of total – and even totalitarian – explanation, exploration and investigation, and the real task of theory is to complicate the object.

RB *We play, but we do not understand that we are playing.*

At bottom, yes, what we are involved in is a game – with rules, not in mastery, laws, protocols of knowledge and so on. But I don't mean to claim that this is a particularly special or original position. I believe a great number of philosophers do something other than just philosophise. Everyone finds themselves confronted sooner or later with this kind of enigma of the object. Obviously, a great part of thought is trapped in the identification of the subject or the problematic of subjectivity. Now this can be extremely complex and rich: one can go very deeply into subjectivity and see it ramify in all directions. And it gives us psychology and the like. It's very interesting. But perhaps something else is in play.

SL *A question about 'production'. You speak in* Symbolic Exchange *of accumulation, production and stockpiling, which naturally made me think of the Heideggerian* 'Bestand' *in 'The Question Concerning Technology'. And there, for Heidegger, 'production'* [Herstellung] *is part of a series, with representation* [Vorstellung] *subsumed under the notion of* Gestell . . .

'*Stell*' again, yes . . .

SL *I'd like to know what you mean by 'production', not just within that Heideggerian framework, but whether stockpile, accumulation, irreversibility and the idea of 'terms' . . . In* Symbolic Exchange *there are no terms in the same sense . . .*

Ah, yes, in *Symbolic Exchange* there are no 'terms'. That's right. There are no poles or polarisation of that kind. There's a kind of cycle, but can we picture that as involving 'terms'? It is a form, at least.

SL *And the production of an object?* . . .

This is difficult because at the point when I wrote *Symbolic Exchange* the term 'production' was so much in the air. It was such an accepted historical-materialist, Marxist term that there was, in the end, no need to define it. Material production, yes, the production of goods . . . but I analysed this a little more as the production of signs . . .

SL *Of desire?*

Yes. And production of differences, in fact. Perhaps the real system of mastery of the world is the production of differences, that is, bringing terms into being. There is a kind of confusion or indeterminacy of things; to bring forth a distinction or polarisation of terms is a kind of dialectic which allows you to master the game and to neutralise it at the same time, to harness difference. Or alternatively, production can be the act of harnessing desire in objects. The object is also a mode of crystallisation. The object is a difference, as it exists at a particular moment – that is, distinctive, isolated. It is, manifestly, differential. So it enters into a system of a structure of differences. So much for production.

To production I had opposed seduction – seduction being precisely what abolishes this polarisation. Seduction can't be said to be the same thing as symbolic exchange, but there is a paradigm which is more or less the same from the start, whether we're talking about seduction, symbolic exchange, the feminine, death . . .

SL *Expenditure* . . .

But this concept of seduction has been so badly misunderstood that I've more or less given it up. And the same goes for the symbolic. There have been so many misunderstandings about the symbolic, about seduction that . . .

SL *The symbolic too?*

Oh yes. *Symbolic Exchange* was very well received. Very well indeed. But it was received either by reference to the symbolic in Lacan – sometimes as contrasting with his positions – or within a very religious perspective – as being opposed to rationalism and so on. But the way I tried to get out of all that – in the system of reversibility and so on – wasn't clearly understood. There was an awful lot of confusion, which contributed to the success of the book, but did so on a basis that was somewhat dubious. That has often been the case – as it was with seduction. And when we come to the way simulation has generally been taken up by artists and those in the fine arts, then you have a total misunderstanding. But that takes us away from the subject.

SL *Well, if you'll excuse my obsession, can I perhaps bring you back to the question about Heidegger?*

Yes, let's take the question of 'enframing', *das Ge-stell*, and 'The Question Concerning Technology'. For a long time I found that a problem, because the analysis I made of the system and the code and so on could be said to amount, ultimately, to a somewhat Heideggerian analysis – technology as the definitive realisation of metaphysics, a rather nostalgic vision, in the end, of the 'other' of technology. Whereas now, in fact, I'm much more inclined to drop this Heideggerian vision and find a kind of ironic principle of technology. In other words, to pose the question – to which I don't have an answer – of whether technology (and all the system of virtuality and so on) is really the mode of enslavement of the real, the mode of extermination of the real, and thus the total disillusioning of the world, or whether, in the end, technology might not be a detour – a gigantic, but also an ironic, paradoxical detour adopted by the illusion of the world, the radical illusion of the world. So we would be wrong, as it were, about the manifest, official objective of technology and its consequences. Beneath the immense system of technology and all that goes with it, the object – or something of that order – would be there playing out its game, playing its own game and perhaps fooling us into thinking we possess a kind of mastery over it. Then the question takes on quite a different complexion. And there we leave the Heideggerian problematic.

SL *Like Heidegger, you also speak in this book of the extermination of the object in hyperreality, but you believe the object would be in play behind . . .*

Yes. But this is a difficult question, because there will never be any way of verifying. Verification is practically impossible. So we are left once and for all with the ironic situation of two hypotheses which are incompatible but are perhaps both true [*laughter*]. As Wittgenstein says, the world is everything which is the case. There is a kind of ambiguous self-evidence here – entirely ambiguous.

RB *What are the contemporary forms of reciprocity? Are these to be found in the family, in . . .?*

No. I don't see this in psychological or relational terms any longer. Or micro-individual or inter-individual terms. It's my impression that there is reciprocity in what might best be termed the zone of impossible exchanges. There's symbolic exchange. And then there's commodity exchange, on the basis of equivalence, which is not the same thing at all and does not involve reciprocity. So reciprocity is to be found, then, in forms of impossible exchange – exchanges which are impossible for our system.

I've analysed exchanges between terrorists and hostages – the type of relation where there is a terrible reciprocity, where reciprocity takes violent, almost unacceptable forms.

RB *But isn't terrorism beyond reciprocity?*

No, I believe that somewhere, in a certain kind of violence like that, one precisely gets beyond the confrontation between subject and object, persecutor and victim. This is what Bataille talked about as well . . . You get back to this sort of continuity of the cycle of reversibility. You find it in Bataille's concept of continuity too. This sometimes takes material form. As for precise cases, I cannot say. But between terrorists and hostages or persecutors and victims, there is a form of exchanging of roles, a role reversal. It was Eric Gans, an American who has made an analysis of that kind, who said: 'We can only grasp the secret of human destiny if we can grasp, in all its horror, this confusion of persecutor and victim.' And I think, on this same model, we can only grasp the sense of human mind if we can grasp in all its irony this coincidence of subject and object.

RB *So there is nothing beyond reciprocity. The difference between Bataille and yourself is that, for you, there is nothing beyond reciprocity?*

Yes. It was only afterwards that I began to think about this, but Bataille's general economy is still too economic. Equivalence is transgressed, with 'expenditure' and all that, but the basic concepts are still those of production or overproduction, of the necessity to spend, to find the accursed share. Whereas in reversibility everything is 'accursed share' or there is no 'accursed share', since there is no residue. We can take an example from *Symbolic Exchange*, namely the example of the analysis of poetic language, where there is no residue, nothing left over, since everything is exhausted in the reciprocity of terms, in the reversibility of terms – or in Saussure's anagrams. At this point, in this set-up (we can't call it an economy any longer), we are entirely beyond economics and even beyond Bataille's general economy, which is all the same a kind of prodigality, of resolution by prodigality of the problems of political economy. This is more or less how it is. Bataille seems to me quite brilliant by comparison with the way classical political economy poses problems, naturally, but he still seems relatively caught in the trap of economics. I don't say this by any means as a criticism or a rejection. It's not that.

SL *Perhaps we can come back to something you spoke about yesterday and which fascinated many people: your comments on morality.*[2] *I have a question about morality, but it is also perhaps a question about your pessimism or optimism, though I'm not exactly sure about this. Currently, in Britain, there's a great vogue for Levinas, which has been going on for about a year . . .*

We have the same phenomenon in France, though perhaps over the last two years . . .

SL *And yet he's been around for fifty or sixty! . . . What interests me here – I quite like Levinas, but in a sense I'm a bit against him – is that there's a pessimism in Levinas in that, for him, what exists is of the order of the 'There is' but not of the* 'Es gibt'. *When I reread* Symbolic Exchange *a few weeks ago, having read it many years ago in French, there seemed to be some* 'Es gibt' *there, since there is either the gift or alternatively a generosity, a plenitude, the possibility of a fullness. Whereas in Levinas everything is empty and this seems pessimistic. So how are we going to find an ethics, a morality? . . . Yesterday you said we mustn't create a morality based on the subject. This is now the wrong tack . . .*

Yes, if I can just interject something here. We didn't have enough time to talk about this yesterday. Effectively, as a subject (and even if we take the theoretical option of analysing the object, we remain subjects), it is impossible – at that subject level – not to have a morality. But, in my view, there's an inevitable dissociation here. Even without bringing in Descartes' double morality, everyone has two levels of this kind. At least we have to speak of another level where morality no longer exists, where things are analysed in a way that goes beyond morality. And not just in

Nietzschean terms – which would involve, as with Bataille, the idea of a 'beyond' of, or transgression of, values, a transvaluation of values and so on – but if we are in the space of the object (the space of what there is on the other side), the refraction of that space is not at all the same any more and there the question of morality can't even arise. This is the case with the space of the current news media. There is always a problem about the ethics of news reporting (do we need a media code of ethics and so on?), but it is a false problem since there's no relation between these two things: there's no possibility of a relation between the news media, as they actually function, and the transcendence of a morality. The news and information media function by contiguity, by capillarity, by a kind of total metonymy, but there isn't the slightest possibility in all that of a moral metaphor, a moral transcendence, and so on. The two things can't be connected. It's a false problem.

SL *But a morality without transcendence, an ethics without transcendence? An ethics of symbolic exchange surely has nothing to do with transcendence. It's a rooted ethics, an ethics not governed by the law, but by rules – governed by practices, not by laws . . .*

Or one can make a distinction – as I do – between values and forms. I am not speaking of a morality which bears on values, because I don't believe in a morality of that kind any more. But there are also forms. And they are something quite different. Values are perishable; they are dying away. We can at least take the view that there's nothing more to be had from a system of values. But, in my opinion, *forms* are indestructible. By forms, I mean things like seduction, challenges, reversibility. Reversibility, in particular, is a form. And it doesn't give rise in any way to a *moral* principle of action; it's a form, and what we have here is play. Forms are something which we play out – at the level of illusion and 'the rules of the game', and so on. And obeying the rules of a game is not a morality, but simply conforming to the game itself. It's not a matter of saying I accept or reject the rule. I play, and if I play there is an immanent rule. Not a rule that is defined as something elsewhere, as something transcendent to the game. It *is* the game: the way or play [*jeu*] of the world. And if I am in that game – at the level of appearances and so on – then there is no law or morality in that. But that is not to say that this is immoral in the diabolical, 'bad' sense of the term. Nor even in the Nietzschean sense, perhaps. It is something self-evident: the self-evidence of the rule. There can be behaviours, then, or even a whole culture organised around this form of illusion and reversibility. It will not be moral in the sense we were speaking about. But the difficulty is avoiding the kind of immoral pessimism there may be in not accepting that. It's always being said that I'm pessimistic, nihilistic and so on. But this isn't a nihilism, because there is in it a kind of acceptance – not acceptance in the sense of being resigned to something, but a taking on board – of what is self-evident, of what is the rule. This is neither optimism nor pessimism. It's the game. And the pleasure of the game. It is not at all nihilistic.

RB *Are we talking of a local or a universal game?*

It can be all kinds of local games – very fragmented, very fractal, very intermittent. It can also be conceived – though it must be stressed that it isn't a metaphysics – as *le jeu du monde*: the 'play' of the world . . .

SL *To come back to the earlier question. The morality you speak of, the subjectless morality – well, not entirely subjectless, but not subject-based – which is in rules, in games, is a little Wittgensteinian. This puts me in mind of the neo-Aristotelians, people like Charles Taylor and MacIntyre . . .*

Or gaming and the *differend*. There's Lyotard too.

SL *Even Foucault at the end.*

Yes.

SL *When I read your descriptions of symbolic exchange, I think of classical, medieval society and read them, for example, as casting light on that. But in our present society things are not so fixed and distinct. Where are we to find the possibility of these exchanges? They must be somewhere, but where?*

Ultimately, what might be closest to a morality would be a rule of stripping-away [*dépouillement*], the rule of the Stoics. This isn't something positive, so that you'd say: 'There's a value here, you have to behave according to that value.' There is no ideality here, but an indifference on the part of the world and nature. And the only virtue, at bottom, is in not adding *pathos* to the world. In other words, in not adding to desire the *pathos* of desire, not adding to suffering the *pathos* of suffering, and so on. That is what the subject does with value: his transcendence is a kind of adding-weight-to – an increasing – of the world's indifference. The only task, then, would be to clear a space, as it were, around the object, to act so that it shone out resplendent in all its indifference, in its immorality, though not in a negative sense – perhaps amorality would be better – so that the subject himself can attune himself to the world, harmonise with the world in a kind of symbolic exchange of indifference.

Indifference circulates because indifference isn't nothing, it isn't negative. It is, perhaps, a passion. At all events, that's what it could be said to be for me. Perhaps even the fundamental passion. And so far as that passion is concerned – a passion being a dual relation, a circulation of things – perhaps the closest ethical world could be said to be that of Stoicism. But that isn't really a historical reference for me; Stoicism isn't the origin of my position, nor is it what I come back to, but there is an affinity.

It's true, however, that this question of morality or immorality is often reduced to a value judgement, which consists in saying: you are pessimistic, you are nihilistic, and so on. It's often resolved in terms of optimism or pessimism. The whole of morality ultimately consists in believing that it is possible to be moral. Morality is founded wholly and solely on this moralistic *petitio principii*. And you're not forgiven for questioning this. I've not been forgiven for this: for not according value, for not adding value to something, to some particular process, and ultimately for offering no kind of solution, opening or ideal, or the like. In that sense, I am indifferent. Not nihilistic but indifferent. And I believe there is philosophy only after you have succeeded in setting aside this kind of presupposition of value. But that is unpardonable, unacceptable . . .

RB *At what level are we to understand this concept of indifference?*

Well, though I've given the example of Stoicism, I'm not talking about that kind of philosophical indifference, but about indifference in relation to our current *pathos*, our current system. And our system is a system of non-differentiation [*indifférentiation*] too. It too – the system of coding and decoding of information, of virtuality – puts an end to this kind of dialectic of terms. It is beyond that. Simulation is nothing less than the abolition of the opposition between true and false, good and evil, and so on. So, simulation is obviously not the false; it is the neither-true-nor-false. The whole system is a kind of realisation of indifference, almost a form of indifference incarnate.

Now, obviously, it's not the indifference of seduction or of symbolic exchange; it's something short of that. In a way we might be said to have realised Nietzsche's transvaluation of values, but to have realised it not 'beyond good and evil', but, sadly, 'this side of good and evil'. We have to come to terms with this situation. However, the rule must be not to try to escape this kind of profound indifference of the system by retrieving value and difference, but to try to play with this indifference – this objective indifference which is our destiny – to manage to transform this fateful indifference into the rule of the game, if not indeed play with it. And to recover a sort of passion for indifference. Isn't the new register, the new space of a new form of game to be found in indifference itself, which is in theory the opposite of all passion?

Now, gaming is a passion. If we rediscover either the cards or the rules of the game, we rediscover the possibility of playing or gaming. The problem – and it is a paradox – is that, as you might say, we have the cards – a certain number of cards to play with – but we don't have the rules. That, in fact, is more or less how I see it. And what do I do? I deal out a few cards, but I can't provide the rules. I don't know them myself. Or, alternatively, you might say that we have the rules, but we don't have the cards. That's true of thought, perhaps. At a particular point, you can find a kind of . . . not the key to the mystery, but the space of the mystery. But we don't have the cards, because all the cards have been stolen by the system. It's the system that holds all the cards. So we never have both the cards and the rules at the same time, if I can put it this way. This is a situation which is, for the moment – and doubtless irreversibly – irresolvable. And this situation of irresolvability is tragic, if you like, but not dramatic. It isn't pessimistic. It isn't nihilistic. Quite the opposite: it is *the* situation and, in that sense, it is an original one.

So we shouldn't attack the system negatively any more or critically take it to task for not giving us the cards to play with, because that seems to me entirely nostalgic and pessimistic – nihilistic: the essence of nihilism. We have to transform it. It's a bit like Borges' 'Lottery in Babylon',[3] where chance, randomness (which is the very opposite of freedom) transmutes itself into the rules of the game – that is, we have to find the possibility of playing in the very impossibility of being ourselves. In my view, this kind of operation isn't exceptional; it isn't the preserve of theorists: you can try and do it in thought, but in my opinion people in their lives do it every day. It's the game of life.

When I said yesterday we are all terminals, that was a logical description of the system itself; but I believe and hope – otherwise I wouldn't even speak – that philosophy and art have no special privileges here. In terms of neurons – intelligence and knowledge, and so on – there's a profound inequality, of course, but where symbolic exchange, reversibility and the rest are concerned, everyone has the same potential. Everyone is equal before the rule. We are not equal before the law, of course: the law is a principle of profound inequality. But everyone is equal before the rule because it is arbitrary. So there we find the foundations of a true democracy, if I may put it like that, though not by any means of the usual political type.

SL *I've a lot of sympathy for your position, but I'm not sure I understand these 'terms' . . .*

There's a possible confusion. It's true that today everything circulates. But there are no longer any terms, there is no longer *the* terminal, *the* network. What we have is the circulation of the network and the circuit, if I may put it like that. We're no longer in the realm of that kind of indefinite metaphor which, for example, means that in the symbolic exchange between human beings there's a form of symbolic transfusion of forms between them – animals, men, nature and so on – that whole cycle which went round and round, where forms were transformed into each other.

Today, what we have is pure circulation, which is that of the pure network, where there are no longer even any forms. The circulation of the network is the circulation of formulas, if I can put it that way. It's playing on words a bit, but what we have here is no longer a form, but a formula – the highly simplified coding of information, and so on. And, where this circulation is concerned, there's no possibility, for example, of stopping. That's the problem: we have lost even the secret of stopping things, of halting them. But symbolic exchange always implies the possibility of death, of stopping, falling still, being suspended. With symbolic exchange, there's a whole dramaturgy. On the other hand, with the network and circulation on the network, there's no dramaturgy. It's not metaphor any more, but metabolism. This is very different, and yet it's true that in neither case are there any longer any terms.

There are, if you like, three possibilities. There is a possibility of a reign of symbolic exchange, in which there is continuity, a cycle and so on; then, there is an intermediary form, as one might put it, which we might call that of terms and the opposition of terms, of meaning, rationality, and so on; then, beyond that, in virtuality, we are once again in a register where there are no terms or poles, where everything is in a form of indeterminacy, but that indeterminacy is not symbolic at all. This is not irreversibility, it is indeterminacy. And there – and this is complicated, since we have to look at some of the most contemporary theories of indeterminacy (chaos theory and so on) – there are many similarities with reversibility and the like, but what we find is not reversibility, but turbulence and indeterminacy. This is all very exciting, but it's a long way from the world of the Enlightenment and reason, from the conventional world of rationality: we are in the fractal, the molecular, the plural, the random, the chaotic. There's a whole world there, but there are no 'rules of the game' in that world. It is in a state of disorder, whereas symbolic exchange is an order. There are rules to it. Though it's true that there may be many resemblances between the two, they should not be conflated.

Otherwise, we come back to the ahistorical, timeless hypothesis that we are always dealing with the same situations, the same forms: things never change; the terms of the exchange are filtered through different technologies, but they are always the same and no radical change has occurred at all. That may perhaps be satisfying for the mind – in the sense of celebrating a timeless spirit – but what's the point of talking about it in that case? We have to start out from the fact that something has happened – a break, a mutation has taken place – and that we are in a new world.

Here I'll defend the idea of 'difference', because we have to cultivate difference a little here, mark the difference. Otherwise, thought is pointless. Thought is, after all, a discourse – *discursus* – and, necessarily, there is difference: at a particular point something happens and things are not the same afterwards. Here, I think, there is a genuine break after modernity. This is perhaps the only case in which we can really take the term 'postmodern' seriously. There has been a kind of break, and I think even the philosophy of the philosophers – and I include Foucault and Derrida in this – doesn't take this mutation (which is very subtle) into account in all its consequences.

And I mean by this that we are now in a different world. This is not science fiction, but I know it perhaps takes a kind of anticipation to sense what this other thing is. We have really passed beyond something, perhaps even beyond the end – I've analysed this question in *The Illusion of the End* – and in fact there is no finality or end any longer, because we have already passed beyond. And there, the rules are no longer the same.

SL *But in* Symbolic Exchange *there are already no finalities . . . For us, in the Anglo-Saxon world, this is perhaps a little difficult to understand, perhaps because we are not clear about what you mean by 'terms' and 'finalities'.*

'Term' is the word for the 'end' in all its ambiguity, because in French, too, the 'term' is the end and the finality – that is, the ideal end of something, which is a bit different. But you can play on the two. Now, in *Symbolic Exchange* there was effectively no finality, but reversibility. And what is reversible isn't final.

SL *The world is not final either . . .*

No, it is a form of reversibility. Extermination certainly is final – extermination, which I was speaking of yesterday and which I take literally as ex-termination. *Ex-terminus*: what has passed beyond the end, so to speak.

Now, in the system of reason and modernity, progress and so on, there is an end, a transcendence, and so on, and we are now beyond that, in a kind of other system which has passed beyond the end. We are not this side of finality, but already beyond finality. This is what I mean when I say everything is realised. We are in the absolute real, so to speak. The virtual is the same thing. And having to make sense of a world where the end is not ahead of us but behind us and already realised changes everything. The whole nature of the problem has changed. This is a hypothesis which seems to me to cast a certain amount of light on all the current impasses of philosophy – the impossibility of rethinking the problem of values, of freedom or utopia, and so on. In France, everyone is trying to find a new basis for political thought, rereading Kant and so on. That seems to me to smack rather of despair.

Translated by Chris Turner

NOTES

1. J. Baudrillard (1993), *Symbolic Exchange and Death*, London: Sage, pp. viii–xiv. [Editors]
2. Published as: J. Baudrillard (1995), 'The Virtual Illusion: Or the Automatic Writing of the World', *Theory, Culture & Society* 12, November, 97–107. [Editors]
3. J. Baudrillard (1990), *Seduction*, London: Macmillan, pp. 150–3. [Editors]

10 Vivisecting the 90s

Interview with Caroline Bayard (CB) and Graham Knight (GK)

CB/GK *Your relation to McLuhan is interesting, the more so since few critics have analysed it, although they have often commented on it. What is the role of the strong presence of the visual, so real in your texts, in relation to the notion of distance, or of obscenity, and in relation to irony as distance? It is clear that the visual would be necessary to separate and distance an imaginary on which sense is founded. But how does one treat the question of the differentiation of image and sound, the latter being a much more supple, fluid, floating medium than the latter?*

I have some difficulty replying to this question because sound, the sphere of sound, the acoustic sphere, audio, is really more alien to me than the visual. It is true there is a *feeling* [word spoken in English] about the visual, or rather for the image and the concept itself, whereas sound is less familiar to me. I have less perception, less analytic perception, of this aspect. That is not to say that I would not make a distinction between noise and sound, but ultimately, in terms of this ambient world's hyperreality, this noosphere, I see it much more as a visualisation of the world rather than its hypersonorisation.

What can I say about the difference between the two? I have the impression that cutting across the world of McLuhan – he too is very much oriented to the visual, of course, in spite of the fact that he was, I believe, a musician – there is a small problem, which is that the different sensorial, perceptual registers tend, in this media noosphere, to conflate, to fuse together into a kind of depolarisation of sensory domains. We speak quite rightly today of the audiovisual; we couple them together in some sort, some kind of amalgam or 'patchwork'. Perhaps I am led to view space in this way by my lesser sensitivity to the acoustic, but it seems to me that everything is summed up in a logistic which integrates all the perceptual domains in a way even more undifferentiated than before. Everything is now received in a manner that is indistinct, virtually indistinct, in fact.

The virtual is the kind of concept that is a bit cosmopolitan, if one can call it that, or postmodern, I do not know. In that respect, it is not about the gaze but the visual; it is not about the acoustic, but the audio. Besides, for McLuhan in fact, everything is ultimately reduced to the tactile. Tactility is really that register of sense which is of the order of contact, not of physical or sensual contact of course, but a sort of communication contact where, right now in fact, there is a short-circuit between receiver and sender. I mean that directly in individual perception, not only in the world of the media but in our bodily way of living, there is a form of indistinction, of amalgamation, of indifferentiation where all the perceptions arrive *en bloc* and are reduced to a tactile ambiance. In the latter there would be a lesser differentiation of registers, a lesser singularity of the gaze, a lesser singularity of sound, of music.

So, that is all one can say. That said, within this state of affairs of course there is perhaps still a way to master the tactile world. I think that McLuhan himself thought so in every way; he thought that there really was a strategy of the tactile world, and that it is not just any one. It is not at all a question of saying that it is insignificant, but simply that it is more undifferentiated.

CB/GK *I remember what you wrote about Westmoreland and Coppola in* Simulacres,[1] *but rereading your text some thirteen years later, I wonder whether the real question may not be somewhere else – if, quite simply, neither one (Westmoreland) nor the other (Coppola) had the last word because there is no such thing as the last word, because history continues, just as stories do, and our history may be just this, a long rewriting process, prolonged ad infinitum, strewn with glosses/counter-glosses. With John Johnston, on the other hand,*[2] *you read history as the re-actualisation of a past in which we are all accusers and defenders, as well as complicitous. Later, in* Cool Memories II, *you interpret it as a stoic temptation, that of a Marcus Aurelius, neither resigned, nor hurried in his late Antiquity, waiting by the sea. Are both those two facets a reflection of your sensitivity? Which of the three is closer to you presently?*

I am not a historian. I do not have an historical perception of events. But I would say that I have a mystical reading of them and that history, for me, would be a long narrative which I tend to mythologise. Curiously, I am going back here to an interesting hypothesis, that of an English naturalist of the nineteenth century, called Philip Henry Gosse, who was a palaeontologist and archaeologist.[3] He was studying fossils found in geological sediments and his hypothesis, as he was a Christian and a reader of the Bible, was that creation had taken place ex-nihilo and the world created as such 5,000 years before his time. Thus God had created at once fossils, geological sediments, exactly as they were in the eighteenth century, and he had created them as simulacra, as a *trompe l'oeil* in order to provide humanity – which might have been traumatised by such a brutal creation – with a history, hence a past. Therefore God would have provided human beings with a retrospective past by creating fossils and geological sediments. And he would have created them as such, with utmost exactitude so that people may study them scientifically, although their past had thus been invented. This brings me specifically to Russell's paradox, which suggests that the world as such could have been created yesterday and everything in it could be interpreted as retrospective simulation. Of course this is a paradox, but for myself I would tend to use such a paradox. This, where one ends up in a real or hyperreal situation, that of the history of historical narratives, of historiography, which do pose a historical question about the reinvention of past history through the historian's discourse, a discourse which by definition is a reconstruction. In a way, that reconstruction is *also* necessarily artificial.

The tendency today is not to regress, but to go back to those moments which preceded that history, as if it were taking us backward, a process which allows questions as cruel as: 'Did the Holocaust actually take place; did gas chambers really exist?' One question, latent within our contemporary imagination, is its incapacity really to understand history, to capture its responsibility, its finality, and therefore to ask such a query which is absurd, but which constitutes the ultimate test about a past event. Did it actually take place? What proof do we have about it?

Of course we have a multitude of objective, real proofs, but what does one do with historical reality in a system which itself has become virtual?

As for history, well I cannot situate it within a realistic framework, nor can I integrate it within a moral, or even political, reference system. There may be a philosophical moral of history, but I do not know what my position would be on that score. It would have to be one of undecidability about what history is, as history today enters into the same domain of indeterminate, undefined interpretations or into the principle of indeterminacy. And this not only applies to the past, but also to the future as well as to the present. At the moment, we live in a sort of uninterrupted time, especially as we move towards the crystallisation of time in each instant, as we keep losing our sense of any objective reference. I do not want to defend history, I only observe a series of problems.

CB/GK *I might be tempted to say that your simultaneously ironic and perspicacious scrutiny of the social and political effects of simulation has been your gift to the end of this century. What made such a scrutiny vulnerable, for some, has not been the epistemological fallibility upon which it grounded itself (as that could be as a demonstration of humility coming from the end of an empire, assuming such is the case with the Western world), but rather, it has been your refusal to recognise that CNN, the Murdochs and Maxwells of this world, dead or alive, do exert a remarkable control over the images which our eyes look at day after day, whatever those media empires' powerlessness to resolve even our most insignificant problems. Yes this did puzzle a number of us. While I do recognise that our referents have been transformed by these images' interaction, I have enormous difficulty in admitting that reference itself could have sunk below the horizon of our collective anomie. Bodies are killed, entire cities, or small towns and communities disappear, between Sarajevo and southern Iraq. No one denies the simulation effect which our information networks rely on, but it is your denial of reality, of personal experience initiated by those simulations which disturbs me. Had you been in Baghdad in February 1991, or in Sarajevo these past two years, might you not have hesitated before casting reference into the dustbin of history?*

Yes, I would not be irresponsible enough to claim an extraterritorial position. When I speak, I do so from a given place. I do have roots. Obviously, all radicals do. I have mine, but those are not ideological references.

Sarajevo, since you are talking about it, reminds me of a media incident, precisely. Bernard-Henri Lévy went there to do a TV programme during one of the worst bombings and he interviewed a woman, a librarian, who spoke to him and said: 'I wish Baudrillard were here to see what transparency really is.' Well, she was doing me a great honour, remembering what I have written about the transparency of evil, the trans-apparition of evil, specifically in a universe which pretends to be a new world order from which evil, at least theoretically, has been eliminated. She felt this was a further illustration of what I have written about the transparency of evil.

Let us talk about this. Such a perspective may arouse a certain misunderstanding. Of course, she is flattering me when she remembers that I have written about the transparency of evil, about the trans-apparition of evil in a universe which defines itself as a new world order, from which evil, at least theoretically, is supposed to be eradicated. One finds oneself within the virtuality of goodness, of positivity, whereas, on the contrary, within such a system evil transpires everywhere. And that is the trans-apparition of evil. Evil is not that through which one sees, but that which sees through everything, which goes through, transpires through good as well. And at that specific time one notices a perverse conversion of all positive effects, of all political constructions, which finally, through some perverse and magical effect, become evil. So that, ultimately, all of those events taking place in Central Europe, the liberation of these countries, Yugoslavia, Bosnia, Sarajevo, are a terrifying demonstration of this catastrophic, recurrent scheme in which evil takes place. And I do not understand evil as suffering, as pain. I define it, rather, as negativity, as the diabolical nature of things when they are reversed into their opposite, so that they never reach their finality, nor even go beyond it and thus become, at that specific time, monstrous. A good part of monstrosity, in our banality, is just that: all phenomena become extreme. Because of the media, our scientific means, our knowhow, progress, all take an uncontrollable, inhuman dimension. Evil, for me, is just that form.

I do not interpret it on the level of experienced pain, in which case I have nothing to say, any more than anybody else, except from a moral viewpoint, but I do not want to consider that. I interpret it not by bracketing it off, but by relativising it. And I can only write while doing this in my own life. But I do not want to be more specific. There is a logic about writing, about thought, about philosophising, yes, a stoic logic in that sense. One cannot add pathos, a subjective dimension, nor a collective sense of things to the vision one may have of the world, as well as of nature. Although, of course, when I say this I am quite aware that such a position is provocative, paradoxical and ultimately unacceptable. I do understand people's anger against such a position. And it is also true that all of this does not leave me indifferent. One can participate physically and morally in collective grief, and since we are talking about this, I also believe that it is a Stoic's duty, if there is one, not to sublimate, not to abstract, not to distance oneself, but to say: such is the rule of the game and this is how I play it. To maintain this ultimate ironic possibility may be the essence of grief, the obsession of grief, the therapeutic obsession to dispose of evil, but those may not constitute the last word of history. I cannot say much more about it although I do recognise that such a position exposes itself to very serious charges.

CB/GK *The question which most easily comes to mind in line with what Caroline was asking you relates to what I would call the 'morning after'. To offer one's eye may well be seductive, overlooking the physical discomfort of the initial moment, but what happens the next day when one finds oneself blind in one eye? Isn't the choice obvious between the suffering of seduction and eternal infirmity? Bodies do obliterate other losses.*

Stories do not have a day after; they are made to be used up. There too, if you take things literally, that becomes unacceptable. Ultimately, right, one is in the realm of cruelty, in a certain sense. And what now could happen the next day if not vengeance? In every respect sacrifice has no final end in that sense. It has no day after, in the sense that it has no end since it reproduces itself. Each extends it. In every way, we know well enough that it is a little game, like money that one wins or loses in a game. Money won in a game does not leave the game. It must be burnt up, consumed like that, in the game. And it seems to be the same thing in a system of gift-giving, of sacrifice, where there is no day after, no point at which one would settle accounts, no point at which one would say: 'So, I have been robbed. I am the loser. I have been sacrificed and I must avenge myself.' No, one keeps on playing. One can perhaps reply to your question, 'what happens the day after?', by saying that at that point one rips out the other eye, and solves the problem!

CB/GK *How is the concept of strategy used? It is implicit that it connotes a form of subjectivity, and yet it is used in such a way that subjectivity is undermined, or placed in a context where it is made volatile or fragile. Moreover, strategy being originally a military metaphor, to what extent does it still retain martial connotations which complicate its sense even more?*

Yes, there I agree with you. The term strategy represents an opportunity because it is apt. It is a nice term. It has form, it speaks to the imaginary. It has a form of mastery and, at the same time, it is deployed within space. But it no longer means anything great in my opinion, because, for there to be a strategy, there has to be a subject of the strategy, someone who has a will, and a representation of the outcome. There has to be a finality. If the strategy has to become logistically chancy, it is no longer a strategy, properly speaking. Thus, one can still use this term in a metaphorical sense, perhaps, but it has certainly lost its military reference, and perhaps even its reference to a finality.

When I use it in the expression 'fatal strategies', it is clear that it no longer has any finality in itself. It is a type of fatal process, a process in which there is certainly no more subject, no more subjectivity. Fatal strategy for me is a strategy of the object. Which means nothing, to be sure! How could an object have a strategy? It would be absurd. But all the same, I like to apply things that are paradoxical. I also speak of objective illusion. Illusion, if it is contrary to a truth principle, cannot be based on objectivity. But I like to bring these two terms together all the same to create a clash between them. Thus fatal strategy is, effectively, an expression which describes a process, a reversibility that is in the order of things, and this is, at the moment, truly delirious, fatal. We are all inside it, but we are nevertheless a vectorial element of the thing, though not in the sense of subjects. At this point it has to be said that this supposes such relativity in the subject–object relation that it is that which becomes fatal.

We witness the loss of subjectivity on the one hand, and the intervention of the object itself in the game in a fatal, decisive and determinant way. And the fact that it is no longer the subject that possesses things when, properly speaking, there is only a strategy of the subject, the fact of speaking of the strategy of objects is a paradox, a kind of metaphorical transfer of things. But as discourse itself is so grounded in subjectivity in this sense, we do not have an objective discourse available in the sense I intend it, which has nothing to do with scientificity, but which would be the discourse of the object. Well, we do not have it. What we have is the event itself, the flow of the world itself, and there is there, if not a strategy, at least a rule of the game. Regardless, I think that there is a rule. But I am not the one who is going to say that. It is truly unreadable; it is a secret. But somewhere there is a logic in the unfolding of things, even if it is a crazy logic. Let us call it strategy. Why not! It is, all the same, the way that the discourse of sense tries to describe non-sense. But, clearly, one will always remain between the two. There will not be any objectivity there in the scientific sense of the term. That is not possible.

CB/GK *It seems clear at this point that a younger generation of philosophers, such as Luc Ferry, Alain Renaut, of social critics such as Michel Maffesoli, or even of less young ones such as Alain Touraine (*Retour de l'acteur, *1988, trans.* The Return of the Actor, *1990; Edgar Morin,*

Pour un nouveau commencement, *1991), have focused on the return of this same subject. Certainly not in the same terms as their humanist predecessors, or their foundationalist ones, but on the subject nevertheless – let us leave it undefined for the moment . . . I found it quite striking that in your* Cool Memories *(1987), you began to sketch some of his/her defining features ('What has been exuberantly demolished is being reconstructed sadly'). Except that, in this particular case, the sadness is yours only and the authors mentioned above do not appear to share your grief. Are you interpreting their efforts as a self-delusional journey? Or alternatively, are you interpreting them as a curious ecological process and a recycling temptation for the end of a century: a bit of postmodernity, a sprinkle of liberalism, a dab of Kantian ethics with, at the end, a solid dose of optimism while facing the grief of the rest of the world? Maffesoli and Ferry are notably more optimistic than their elders; Morin and Touraine are more prudent. What is your position on this so-called return of the subject?*

In Maffesoli's case, you are dealing with a very specific subject, since the latter is inscribing his position within a form of tribality. To me it looks like a tribal resurgence in which the subject has become the expression of a specificity, of a singularity. One observes a tribality and a singularity conjoined, in a way. For myself, I am inclined to think that such tendencies are not residual, but represent an elaboration on or around vestigial elements which may well be alive, which function as the scattered fragments of a totality, a globality capable, in spite of everything, of organising the world and the subject as the convenor of that world. This subject had created a form of philosophy, of the 'becoming-subject' of the world. We do not need to invoke Hegel here, but all the same his texts signalled a certain power, specifically a conceptual power, and as everyone knows it does not exist today. My view is that what you are describing today is a form of reparation, that we are all involved in such reparations today, in the SOS subject, or in the SOS subjectivity.[4] Such a subject, moreover, does not appear to be a divided one, a really alienated one drawing all of its energies from its alienation, but rather a reconstituted one, a re-synthesised one within which you cannot discern this pull, this divisiveness with all the consequences they entail for symbolic and imaginary levels. Such a subject is the standard figure, robot of a reconstituted subject trying to recoup its residual vestiges, or whatever is left of them. It could be an ecological subject, and then one would witness the ecology of the subject, the saving of the subject, since it is quite evident that it has been threatened by a very simple evidence and symptom: the disappearance of its object. If it did not die purely and simply, this subject, as well as that which it pretended to objectify, to master, now presently escapes it just as its position of power, of mastery, escapes it too. That subject is not even supposed to know, to be able to believe in anything – it cannot even believe in itself. And among those who reactivate this subject, who turn it into an actor, even those people know that it has lost its integrity as a subject, its conviction to adhere to its own effort to change the world. It does not believe in it any more. It pretends to; it is a form of strategy, a posthumous strategy. That subject is a survivor and one witnesses the survival of the subject or the revival of the subject. Of course it is all about subjectivity, as it is in the interest of all those disciplines right now – sociology, psychology, philosophy – to save their subject. Then it might be the case that, given the disappearance of this active subject and its passive counterpart, one presently witnesses the effects of a subject which attempts to reconstitute around itself the elements of a willpower, of a vision of the world. I really do not believe this. But this being said, there might be an effect of reinnovation, of renovation after a long period of philosophical, or maybe structuralist, destructuring of the subject. It is not mine, but that does not matter. It may also be possible that we are observing a pendulum effect, the weighing scales tilting one way since in the history of ideas one could witness an internal phenomenon, a reactional one, vis-à-vis the history of the world. Because in fact it appears that the subject is only a vanishing point at the moment, to such an extent that it may have reached its fading point and what you are describing may only be a resurgence in the philosophical world. I certainly do not look on it as a credible phenomenon, not for myself in any case.

CB/GK *Sometime in France, after the socialist victory of 1980, light-years ago in a way, I noticed a very healthy reaction on your part, on that of Lyotard as well (*The Intellectual's Grave*), when you both stressed that intellectuals should not speak in anyone's name except in their own. But such were the times in the early eighties when the Left finally had access to power there. It is also clear that you did express such discomfort in your interview with Shevtsova.*[5] *Nevertheless, some fourteen years later, British and American intellectuals such as Tony Judt and Susan Sontag have enunciated interesting reminders to French intellectuals. They did so without any moralising intent, but firmly. Since you were mentioned, let us talk about the latter. Sontag, in particular, voiced discomfort about the French intelligentsia on the line of fire, if you wish, in Sarajevo where she produced the first act of* Waiting for

Godot. *This otherness which she invoked was a humble, physical choice, a presence which did not force itself, did not operate in a grandiloquent manner, à la Glucksmann so to say (he descended on the burning city for a few hours, just to explain while quoting you, that wars are made, won, or lost on TV). Sontag, with her defiance, is determined to return to that city, to produce this play with actors who want to live, to survive, to play, even if they occasionally need to lie down on the floor as they are too tired, too hungry or too ragged. 'Because I want to finish that play, I had to be there with them', says she. In 1993, it probably is a desperate choice, a form of refusal against the worn-out pragmatism of Vance and Owen, an act deprived of any illusions about our collective cowardice and yet essential to remind a blind Europe it should at least come out of its anomia if it wants Bosnia to survive.*

The questions I would like to ask you are the following: first, the realist abjection you were mentioning in The Illusion of the End, *rather than an insistence upon actual interventions, may well be the acceptance of an inevitability, which does not cost us anything and leaves us prostrated as couch potatoes in front of our screens. Then if people such as Sontag were not doing what they're doing, who would do it? How do you define the role of individuals, be it water engineers, intellectuals, pall-bearers, writers or surgeons in those micro-spaces which presently constellate our planet?*

I would like to agree with you. I would love it if there were the simple possibility to finish off this pain. Because if, when one does what Sontag does, it is with no illusion whatsoever, beyond any objective, independently of any goal, any result, to save – to save what? – whatever it is, a form of conscience, pride, a sort of: 'I do it in spite of everything', then I can see that. And it is a heroic act, in the sense that heroism has always been without illusions. Real heroes are always in that sense tragic. They do not exactly foresee the result of their actions. But that is the same thing, one cannot be heroic alone; in that sense I am almost collectivistic. To me, an act does not have meaning by itself, except in an absurd context. Maybe suicide does, maybe in fact what we are looking at here is a form of suicide. I am not sure. But for a choice such as Sontag's to be meaningful, even if it is without illusion, it has to have repercussions on other consciences, and especially within the conscience of those to whom it is destined, such as the people from Bosnia, or the others.

And this is where the clockwork breaks down, because the absorption of all this by the resonance of the sounding board on which it falls, as it is completely perturbed, falsified, mediatised, this anticipated absorption, through the precession of whatever you do, that is what distresses me. I understand one doing it anyway, to save one's own illusions, the illusion of one's will. But is it meaningful to do it? If there is no intellectual world operating as a sounding board, one which would be in solidarity with such an act and which would be capable of extracting a meaning from it, why do it? If one cannot create repercussions, reverberations for such an act to bring it back within history, so that it were 'an event', then there is no point in doing it. In that sense I would be extremely, not opportunistic, but realistic. It is realpolitik I would invoke and suggest that if one does this, chooses to do this, it has to be an event. Not that it should be important, but it should create a rupture in the information continuum. Did it, or did it not, create a rupture? Everything hinges on this. Otherwise it is hard to assess it as a rupture. Of course, one may entertain the idea that if everyone does one's bit, all of this will produce a primitive accumulation of courage, actions, and will ultimately produce an event. But today I do not believe it. Now we are, as Paul Virilio has put it, living in real time, and real time means fatality. Actions have no antecedent, even when they refer to other revolutionary periods; they do not have any finality, even in a long-term context, as no one knows where this is coming from and it all happens in real time. And such a real time manages to set it all up in a state of total ephemerality. Susan Sontag's act is limited. It cannot operate incognito, it is automatically mediatised, that is for sure. This in itself does not represent a radical objection, but it points out a tendency. Information is not what it used to be a long time ago. In the past, something would take place, then one would know it had taken place, then others would hear about it. Now, one knows everything before it has even taken place, and incidentally, it does not even have the time to take place. Mediatisation is a precession, you could call it the precession of simulacra within time. One is in a world where, in order to respond to a reality, to the importance of things, one needs to be far ahead. In an extreme way, one would need to precede the precession itself, to anticipate those simulacra, otherwise the clockwork, the system, will be present before we are there. The simulacra will be ahead of us everywhere.

This was the situation of the Prague student and his double. His double was always there before him. Whenever he would go and meet someone, for a duel for instance, the other had come before him, his adversary had already been killed. So there was no reason for him to exist. We now live in such a system. Can one move forward? In a global situation, one is hostage, complicitous even, with such a situation.

Such is the effect of the Stockholm syndrome: in such events, victims and executioners become in some way complicitous. It is monstrous, but real. Between the hostage and hostage-takers a form of complicity establishes itself.

In order to be able to have a bearing on that immediate event, which is already devoid of its meaning, one would need to be far ahead of the game, in a state of extraordinary anticipation. One can try to do so, through one's intellect or one's writing, although today it is remarkably harder to do so in practical terms. Sontag's gesture, and this is not a value judgement, or a judgement on her courage, because there was a real virtue in doing what she did, but virtues are something else. Strategically, if one uses that word, then there I would be more cynical. There is division of labour that should be respected. Even if there are any intellectuals left – and I am not sure I am one of them, even if I appear to share in such a life, appear to share a specific discourse – I do not share in that complicity of intellectuals who perceive themselves as responsible for 'something', as privileged with a sort of conscience-radicalness that used to be the privilege of intellectuals and now it has been moved on to another space. Subjects such as Susan Sontag cannot intervene any more, even symbolically, but once again this is not a prognosis or diagnosis.

CB/GK *Would it be possible to say that the hyperreal is a state where there is too much reality and not enough ideology? Have we become ideological paupers? Not in the sense that we still believe in it, in fact rather the opposite, in the sense that it used to be our alibi, our excuse on the terrain of subjective irony, something in fact in which not to believe. Interestingly, it has even become difficult to be cynical these days!*

Yes, it is true, since in every respect nobody believes in it any longer. And there lies the problem, when nobody believes in it any more. And not only in relation to ideology, but to indifference as well. Indifference was a fantastic quality, something almost stoical. It was very good to be indifferent in a world which was not, where there were differences, conflicts. So this kind of indifference, a strategy of indifference, created a privileged situation. But in a world that has become completely indifferent, what would it serve? It would be necessary to become different again in order to differentiate oneself from a world which has, objectively, become indifferent. That history is very pernicious.

It is the same thing for art with its power of illusion. What does this become in a world which itself ends up being totally illusory, even random? It becomes very difficult to find a form of intervention like that. So ideology . . . yes, the world is now so totally ideologised, where everything passes through the narrative of ideology, that it no longer serves any purpose to have any. Out of that follows the situation, the transcendence if you like, of ideology which actually, in fact, no longer exists.

I had an experience with simulation and the simulacrum. Nowadays I have had enough of it – twenty years of it, or almost, is enough! Something interesting happened to me recently on this subject, in relation to Japan. There was an erudite Japanese who had come to interview me and I asked him why, when for a number of years he had been translating my books, I had not received any word of it. I had been translated there several times before, and I had been told at that time. 'Ah, simulation and the simulacrum! In Japan you are an important spokesman.' So I asked him why I no longer heard about readers' reactions and he told me, 'But it is very simple, very simple you know. Simulation and the simulacrum have been realised. You were quite right: the world has become yours . . . and so we no longer have any need of you. You have disappeared. You have been volatilised in reality, or in the realisation of hyperreality. It is over. In terms of theory, we no longer need you, and there is no longer a need to defend your theories.' That is the paradox of utopia made real; it clearly makes every utopian dimension perfectly useless.

So I do not know if that answers your question, but ideology seems to me now to be so old a word that in some respects I do not even like to talk about it. In short, if it were true what Marx said, that it is the effect of a reaction of the superstructure on the infrastructure, a mode that reflects the conflictual relation of superstructure and infrastructure . . . but clearly one can no longer give it a fundamental interpretation today except to produce a referential discourse which itself no longer has the effect of a real *clash* in the reality of the infrastructure, but is the legacy of a conceptual discourse that is already archaic/ancient. It becomes a kind of ideological zombie of itself, an artefact of itself. But then, without knowing it because everybody eventually takes up the language of ideology, everybody ideologises things, it becomes our anchor.

As for me, I believe deeply that no one truly believes in it any longer at all. But it will always be there, and that is still the role, unfortunately, of the intellectual class, the political-intellectual class, which maintains the fiction of ideological discourse. Everyone pretends all the same to consume it, since otherwise there would be panic. But at a profound level all this has no more credibility. This is what makes everything suddenly collapse, some day or other. It is a collapse that takes place because for a long time there has no longer been any credible basis to the thing at all. We have always wondered why, in the East, everything happened so fast, without, apparently, any possible foreshadowing of the collapse. Well, it is simply that everything had been completely devitalised for a long time, and the discourse was no longer anything more than a parody of itself. Eventually, a reality that is only a parody of itself will cave in without resistance. There is not even any need to give it a push. Moreover, this new type of event is interesting, arising effectively out of indifference and no longer out of a will to action, but out of a long inertia which has sapped the system. And then, sooner or later, it implodes.

CB/GK *Given the allusions to the Manichaean nature of your strategy, irony is a rather isolated term here. It functions well with parody, but the latter hardly appears in your texts. Why not? Is it because the contradiction between them is already contained within irony?*

You say parody does not appear very much? Though I like the term well enough, parody is still perhaps a little too theatrical, too specular, in spite of everything. The parodic still has a certain power. It is true that I use the term irony a lot more – and what is more, I do not use it in the subjective sense any more. It is no longer subjective or romantic irony, nor humour in that sense. Rather it is a form of irony that is pataphysical, but objective. Before, it was subjective irony. It was to some extent connected to critique, to a critical, romantic, negative point of view, to a form of disillusion. The new irony seems to me rather to be an excess of positivity, of reality. And that is why I call it 'pataphysical', because pataphysics, Alfred Jarry's Ubu, is precisely that. It is the too full, the too much of itself, it is an absolute, total over-awareness, positivity without fault. Ubu's big gut will clearly explode one day. And that is metaphysical irony, the irony of our world, and it is related to a kind of protuberance and excrescence of the system. It is no longer ridiculous in the classic theatrical sense, it is pataphysical. Ubu swallowed his own superego.

Everything is at the same time untouchable and non-existent, and that is the irony of non-existence, of insignificance. It is more radical than the Other. The Other was still, and that, moreover, is what gave it beauty and charm, complicity in the object, whereas irony now pertains to events themselves. The events in the East, where all of a sudden, at a time when one could have believed in the fall of capital, we witness the fall of communism. And that seems to me to be an ironic event, perfectly unforeseeable, and nevertheless dependent on a fantastic logic. It is that irony, rather, that I would insist on now. But it is difficult to thematise because it no longer lends itself to laughter, nor even to a smile really! Perhaps there is an object somewhere that smiles, but we do not know it.

CB/GK *There are times when you almost speak as an Albigensian.*

An Albigensian, yes a Manichaean. Certainly Manichaean in *The Transparency of Evil.*

CB/GK *There is a paradox which captures my attention in all this. On the one hand I hear a certain Albigensianism, which sooner or later is read as a form of prophetic interpretation – it could be Jeremiah in the Old Testament, or even Job on his garbage heap – on other occasions you almost sound like Ecclesiastes. The paradox, for me, hinges around the fact that while I know you feel a perfect repulsion for moralistic rigorism, is it possible to behave as a prophet, especially as accurately as you have sometimes turned out to do without being also a rigorous moralist?*

Rigorous . . . yes, to an extent that is a quality, although rigorism is a flaw, rigour, an extreme rigour is a strength. I would be in favour of extreme rigour. Radicalism is also a form of rigour as well. A rigorous logic seems to be necessary. Pity, and mercy towards reality are not exactly my choice. I would rather go in the opposite direction. And in a way that is true, this could be perceived as a prophetic moralism. Prophetic . . . well, I am not sure, I guess one can extrapolate. In a way, I love to extrapolate, take an idea to its utmost limit, to its extreme. Is this being prophetic? Sometimes it happens to be right, but not necessarily. I do remember that someone tried to make an inventory of all the inane comments I had made – well maybe not inane, but at least illusory – and they had found quite a few. It was a newspaper which had done this, I think it was the *Globe-Hebdo* or some such publication. In a way, it provided me with some publicity for things which had indeed taken place. But I had not uttered those prophecies out of a moralistic sense, although I am not sure whether I am devoid of it – I might have inherited some from my ancestors, who were peasants. So my rigour would be of such a kind. It might come from a sense of repulsion, rather than moralism. Indeed I may be moral in the sense that everything I describe, I do from a sort of distance, cynicism, objectivity, and from a paradoxical stance. I do entertain deep repulsions, simultaneously with some attractions. Of course morals are being sustained by resentments and repulsions. And I must confess that I do feel an objective repulsion towards a number of things. In order to describe something you need to be nasty, to be propelled by the energy of repulsion. The Beaubourg architecture, the Beaubourg aesthetics aroused that in me and I described them with a degree of loathsomeness. But ultimately, when one ends up giving the object its monstrous dimension, its scale or scope strikes you. And in order to find them or to express them, you need to absorb this object and identify with it as well as reject it, violently even. Writing also comes from that locus. It is an acting-out, as we were saying yesterday. Morals also reprove, reject, forbid, although I am not certain that the analogy holds the same primitive reference, that the primitive scene would be the same.

CB/GK *If you had to describe yourself, today, in a quick shot, would you describe yourself as* The Accidental Tourist *of the end of this century: little luggage, few illusions, and gifted with that psychic stoicism the end of a millennium leaves us with at dawn?*

Tourist . . . well that's not very positive. I guess a form of speculation, a capacity for crossing, traversing, yes. A tourist goes through, demonstrates a certain transversality, no doubt, goes to the end of things, or around them. If going around an object or looking at it from multiple viewpoints defines the tourist, then yes that is true. But there is also the fact that tourists avoid, let go, abandon a number of belongings, and I did strive to do that. Why? Because I was probably the happy owner of valuable gear and I tried to get rid of it. I tried not to refer to all of the history of ideas, philosophy even, to all of that richness I admired the most. Somewhere they are still close to me, but I did try not to make reference to them. I chose to forsake them, to abandon objects, that is true. Did I try to create a power vacuum? I do not know whether the term tourist has that meaning, but it invokes a comparable mobility, the absence of primitive, or secondary accumulations, that is me. I tried to avoid accumulations, rather than lean towards expanding. I am not a gambler, not a spendthrift, but one needs to be able to sacrifice in order to recreate a vacuum, and not the other way around, that is clear.

CB/GK *I was thinking about* The Accidental Tourist *when asking you this question, as in* Cool Memories *you delineate beautiful meanders around the subject of exile, which you describe as a wonderful and comfortable structure, marked by unreality and the end of the world.*

Have you been looking for those as fragments to be reached outside of a France filled with greyness and chagrined indecisiveness?

Exile, yes of course. I am quite aware that I operate from a prejudiced position against nationalism, one which is anti-nationalist, or even anti-cultural. Somewhere within me there is a distancing away from what is closer to the bone, for that which is closer to one's own culture, one's country, family is that from which one cannot escape. Such a promiscuousness I perceive as dangerous, and therefore I have always tried to distance myself from it, sometimes with some partiality about what is closest to me. And yet I do value intimacy, roots, ancestry. It is maybe because I have those roots within me that I can afford to become the perfect cosmopolitan, since I know I will always have that form, that substance which solidity confers on oneself and that I will never lose those elements. Therefore I never look on the world as a lost object and I can afford to lose sight of it, especially that which is closer to me, territory or country. That is true as far as France is concerned, where I have always had an anti-cultural prejudice; clearly, I have never forgiven culture, it contains too many unacceptable elements and the world becomes increasingly unacceptable because it 'culturalises' itself at full speed. Everything has now turned into culture, and it has even become very difficult to go beyond one's own culture since one finds it everywhere. There will even be a moment when one will not be able find any deserts. Deserts are a metaphor for disappearing objects, evanescence beyond culture. Now they have become increasingly culturalised they are virtually impossible to find.

Patagonia has become a new frontier, and absence as much as the locus of absence has become extremely difficult to access. The real danger, that is true, is to end up wallowing in an obsessional negativity vis-à-vis the others' culture and the rest of the world. And it is true that I have developed my own biased distance, but I think it is better that way, rather than the other way around.

CB/GK *In the interviews you have given, from Paris to Australia via California, you often speak of the cinema, of the plastic arts, architecture, painting. What place do the other four senses occupy in your life – taste, smell, touch, hearing?*

Ah, we have almost come back to the opening question! How shall I put it? I have not had any musical culture, or acculturation to music, practically none. These are things which later on, in adulthood, you definitely miss. As for painting, the situation was a little bit autodidactic, but ultimately there I know where this is all coming from. Cinema much more, because I really was a bit of a cinema fan at a certain point in my life, while I am much less so today because I no longer happen to find myself there and no longer see what it is any more, that is true. And then, lastly, architecture? Yes, that much more so because of friends in architecture, because of a milieu I knew well, though not through any initial intervention on my part. And so, then, I have finished up with photography, which was and still is exactly a register which is completely intimate and profound for me. Not a profoundness of substance, but perhaps on the surface, though very intense all the same. I have not practised it for very long, perhaps a dozen years, which makes photography as intense for me as writing, though in a completely different way. Yet perhaps it has given me pleasures even more intense than writing.

Is it a relationship with an image, and can you call it an image? For me it is perhaps something else. It is more magical than the real thing. It is the object that, right from the start, has deeply intrigued and obsessed me. I began with the object, after that perhaps the Object with a capital letter, or even the metaphysical object which can be anything one wishes, then perhaps the object as radical otherness, like radical exoticism. For me, the photographic image is a little bit like that, and that is different from cinema. I am not the only one to think that the photographic image is superior to the cinematic image because cinema, in relation to photography, is a loss in terms of illusion, the power of illusion. Of course, it is a progression, an objective one if you like, but like all progress it can very well be precisely, objectively, a loss. Cinema itself, right inside its practice, has lost the force of illusion. It has lost it through colour, by all the improvements that have been made which have, in fact, always seemed highly problematic to me. So the photographic image restores a sort of absolute moment. What Barthes says about it is very nice, though perhaps too nice. I have not really thought about it. It is a raw element, evidently, and I try to keep it that way – harsh – and to practise it harshly, a dimension I recognise quite willingly. For the other senses, even art and painting, I have never been involved in them except at a remove, and rather episodically. I have never really addressed things from that point of view, although sometimes I have found myself involved in these spaces in spite of myself, with New York artists and the Simulationists. And that was an extremely ambiguous adventure. I found myself taken in there like a referent, a referential hostage. I was badly treated. One minute I found myself praised to the skies, and then cut down maliciously. Fine, none of that was my doing. It was an unwitting destiny.

Choice, desire, investments, these would be in the area of the image, effectively in the domain of the image, and more precisely in that of photography. I cannot really explain why; it is where I have found a sort of, not alternative, but a total alternation with writing. Not to have anything but writing makes you really an intellectual, even if you do not like it all the same. Writing is, nonetheless, related more to discourse while photography can be done with a total singularity that is external, alien. Of course there is still a danger there that people end up identifying you as a photographer anyway, and then you find yourself co-opted once again. But for the moment, things are still OK!

NOTES

1. J. Baudrillard (1994), *Simulacra and Simulation*, Ann Arbor: University of Michigan Press, pp. 59–60. [Editors]
2. M. Gane (1993), *Baudrillard Live: Selected Interviews*, London: Routledge, pp. 156–64. [Editors]
3. J. Baudrillard (1996), *The Perfect Crime*, London: Verso, pp. 20–4. [Editors]
4. The term SOS was used in the context of social and political activism. For example, SOS Racisme, an organisation founded by Harlem Desir concerned with combatting racism against non-European immigrants, mobilised considerable attention.
5. M. Gane (1993), *Baudrillard Live: Selected Interviews*, London: Routledge, pp. 72–80. [Editors]

11 Things Surpass Themselves

Interview with Florian Rötzer (FR)

FR *Recently you were criticised as the prototype of an 'administrator of theoretical emptiness' who has taken up a depoliticised position. Not long ago you yourself wrote that today every critical radicality has become useless. Why?*

I don't mean useless, but pointless. We've already run through the entire cycle of critical thought. My earlier books were still thoroughly critical. But since *Symbolic Exchange and Death* I've entered into another discourse, even though this book is still critical in so far as there is in it a desire for a symbolic exchange. The hypothesis of simulation was also still critically meant in the sense that in it there was a Situationist inheritance, and it proceeded from the existence of alienation. But from then on there is no longer a desire for another order or for a subversion in the true sense. The symbolic order was transcended, and the critical perspective was left aside. The critique slipped to the side by itself, not out of any decided intention.

FR *But why do you think critique is meaningless?*

I think it's meaningless in the sense of its functioning within our modern systems. We know that every critique, every opposing force, only feeds the system. At least we've experienced it in that way, and we've had this experience in praxis as well as in theory. For me it's now a matter of transition from a perspective of the subject to that of the object, from which there is no longer any critique. The field of objects is that of seduction, of fate, of fatality or another strategy. For critique, one must preserve the standpoint of the subject with all of its strategies. And precisely these strategies seemed to me to be obsolete and exhausted. But that's more a challenge than a fact or a definite philosophical standpoint. It seemed better to me to go beyond the field of the subject and to speak from the object, if that's somehow possible. That's perhaps an impossible standpoint, but we must keep it in mind and entirely leave aside the standpoint of the subject.

FR *But doesn't this continue the wish for subversion, in which you attempt to assume a standpoint that cannot be integrated into the system? Don't you then remain critical?*

Yes, of course, as soon as one is concerned with language, with discourse, one remains critically placed. One must bring this into play in the sense of an engagement. It's an unstable or metastable critical perspective. When we have to deal with language, there is always a subject, but the endeavour consists precisely in disavowing this subject.

FR *So your endeavour consists not in decentring or dissolving the subject, but in disavowing it.*

Yes, one can observe this in language itself, as, for example, in humour language functions by itself through a power of increase or its own materiality. Then it functions outside the subject. That would be, for me, the standpoint of a position that is ironic and objective at the same time, and also that of the present theory. But I leave it entirely undecided whether my discourse is critical. One can interpret it critically. One never knows whether one has successfully gone beyond one's critical shadow, but I've made an attempt to do that.

FR *You are also not developing a theory about states of affairs in the classical sense, but your writing is more of an experimenting with or a trying out of hypotheses.*

Yes, certainly. And the leitmotifs of simulation, seduction or fatal strategies should also be understood in this way. They are not concepts but rather hypotheses and metaphors that run off in spirals and not in a critical continuum or a dialectic.

FR *Then are your writings meant more as a literary discourse or as games with thoughts? And to whom or to what do you want to appeal with them?*

I must deny the aesthetic characterisation. It isn't literature and it isn't a frivolous play. I would like it to appear serious, to be a theory, but not one that reflects the objective – rather one that is a challenge to reality, to the principle of reality. It is certainly not a matter of a critical theory, but it is not for that reason a type of literature. There must be another game, with other rules, in which truth is still spoken about but in another sense. The content, to be sure, is volatilised more strongly and does not come into play so frontally as in a critique.

FR *You write that traditional theories have lost their objects, and also that the attempt to find or invent truth would no longer work today. You declare: away with truth; it only complicates the game!*

My theory conforms to its own object. When I speak of simulation, my discourse is simulatory; when I speak of seduction, the theory is also a seduction. Thus it comes nearer to its object. And when I speak of fatal strategies, the theory is fatal. There is no longer a standpoint of the subject, but object and subject play with one another. That is no confusion, but a fusion of points of view. Whether it succeeds or not, I don't know.

FR *Do you teach sociology in Nanterre?*

Yes, unfortunately.

FR *Do you understand yourself really to be a sociologist or more of a philosopher?*

Oh, that's always the critical question. I can't actually answer it. I'm certainly not a sociologist in the strict academic sense, and I'm also not a philosopher. Today in France a restaging of philosophy is certainly being carried out.

FR *By Lyotard, for example?*

Yes, him too. I mean that all of these disciplines have already had their day. We've had done with them in the sixties and seventies. I can't understand why we should turn back again. It's not an inheritance because we didn't do any finished work. I mean that this postmodern – I don't know if this word means that – this conjuring up of old disciplines is nonsense. I would like to go further and more quickly beyond them, more than this ghostly preservation.

FR *You spoke before about a Situationist inheritance. In what connection do you stand with Situationism?*

I've always had the tendency to radicality, and I have that in common with the Situationists. We have not thrown away subversion, but in spite of that it's now past. It all came to an explosion in 1968. That was an epoch; it is over, but not radicality. It's still a leitmotif for me.

FR *How can one or should one still be political today?*

Today I'm no longer politically engaged. Transpolitically, perhaps, like Virilio. But we have done away with this political scenario once and for all. The ideas or passions must come from somewhere else today. I see this very well in Nanterre, in this university where everything started, for example with Cohn-Bendit. Today it's an empty field from which nothing more will come – that we know with complete certainty. But that's not something to despair over. We must keep this desolation in view. That's a postulate: it is so! Academic devastation runs parallel to social and political devastation. That's the current reality for us today. The former radicality came from the subject – it was subjective. Today it comes perhaps from the field of the object. Today one can no longer replace the subject; it has played itself out, but naturally not in everyday life. We all still subsist on a kind of banality. But perhaps this banality will also, somewhere and somehow, turn into a certain fatality. That interests me, but not the changes and strategies of the obsolete subject, be it the subject of the political or of knowledge or of history. That is naturally meant paradoxically. There is still no doctrine about it, and one still can't verify it. One cannot foresee what comes from the object. Perhaps it has no consequences; it comes as a pure event or as a pure experience. That is not meant mystically, but something arises there whose track I am on.

FR *Doesn't that mean waiting until objects begin to act, in so far as we can no longer act politically ourselves? Doesn't the position of expectation simply transfer from our own acting to the acting of objects, as a kind of hope that something might yet happen again?*

I'm no prophet. I don't know, I can't know that. For this, I always choose language as a metaphor. One doesn't know what comes from it when it can operate by itself, when the subject pulls itself back. One doesn't know what happens then. It's always surprising and has a deeper intensity than what happens through the subject. It's a question as to what will happen in time. I have no hope and also no illusions. Perhaps there is in this between time, in this epoch at the end of history, or however else one expresses it, even if one cannot take this talk about the end of history or the end of politics entirely seriously, perhaps there is in this time a span in which nothing happens. But we are not discouraged about it. I would like to say one must allow dead time to live. There are such times, and we are experiencing such a time in France right now.

FR *Doesn't this retreat from the political and from critique have something to do with the fact that Mitterrand and socialism are in power in France? Doesn't disappointment set in because utopia has taken place in reality?*

Naturally. There was, at least, no spring, no leap over and beyond anything. The people didn't get anything they were hoping for by putting the socialists in power. However, they had no great illusions, so there is also no real disappointment. What didn't come was a *coup d'éclat.* That must be there, otherwise the people take no pleasure in seeing this or that played out on the political scene. On the contrary, there was only a countercoup. There was no political charm and no seduction, nothing of political energy, no people who knew how to play with the situation or would provoke something. They didn't dare anything. Here a disappointment sets in, but it doesn't touch the content of the political, rather the style. Nothing will fundamentally change in future years. In France, we must live with this desolation of the between time, with this false or simulated metastability in the political and theoretical field. In the United States things have taken a different turn with Reagan. There is an overdimension of banality, of simulated stability there. We don't possess this fourth dimension; we remain in the banality of social and political devastation where even decline has no vitality. What is essential in the fact that we disappear or perish is that there is also an art of disappearing that one has or doesn't have. At the moment we have no style.

FR *You have written about the United States not only that it is the only wild society on earth, but also that the United States would be the land of the future. Therefore, doesn't the talk of disappearing concern more than Europe or the European tradition, which disappears as an independent power in relation to the United States? In the States entirely other political ceremonies are possible. You have compared Mitterrand with Reagan, who can stage euphoria without deception and confusion, while Mitterrand cannot cope with the professionalism of show business in politics. You presumably conceive the affirmative description of this situation as a provocation?*

The transition from the political into what is staged and into simulation as such is entirely banal. The question is whether this happens with a real dimension of modernity, whether it is luxuriously staged or not, otherwise it is petty or affected. What oppresses us is just this affectation in contrast to the United States. There, things take their course entirely of themselves, even when they're simulated. We get this affectation from our petit bourgeois tradition.

FR *Isn't that a very French tendency toward the luxurious? You like to refer to the baroque, where politics occurred as theatre, as staging. In German critical theory – I'm thinking, for example, of Walter Benjamin – fascism was criticised precisely for having aestheticised politics. Isn't that the same thing you demand when you conceive of politics as ritual, as ceremony or as spectacle? Isn't there hidden in this a tendency towards the monumental, which one can also notice in the United States?*

Perhaps it's different there because everything, politics, sexuality and so on, enters into the way of life, is secularised. There is no transcendent religion any more, also no transcendent sexuality; everything is treated with this genius of empiricism. As soon as one has cleansed it of everything transcendent or subjective, then everything works with a certain humoristic genius.

FR *Would this ironic moment be missing, then, in fascism?*

Yes, certainly. But in the United States there is no danger at all of fascism. There is a strange peculiarity with Reagan. Everything is sucked up by publicity staging, and then there is no more opposition. There is nothing in front of him and nothing against him any more. With Reagan and the United States it is like an advertising gimmick. The same thing occurs in the relationship of the United States to the rest of the world. Perhaps America no longer has a monopoly of power as it did in the fifties, but it has become a model and thus no longer has any ideological contrary, any opposition. It has a publicity success, whose symbol was the rise in the value of the dollar, which is not at all understandable. That is a special effect of American power, which is no longer objective, not of weapons, of products, but a power that corresponds to Reagan. That is the full play of simulation. The Americans can play this because they are completely radical in the line of modernity. We have never experienced this modernity, and we are not in this radical modernity today.

FR *But simulation also turns into reality. I'm not only thinking about the possible effects of arms production but also about events like the military occupation of Grenada, which was also a staged political action, or about the relationship to Nicaragua. How can such an action, which has thoroughly bloody consequences, be articulated in the conceptuality of simulation?*

Simulation does not mean there is no violence or death. In the United States there is much violence and great political passions, but that does not result in any concept of history, into which they have not entered at all, just as we have not at all entered into modernity. These are different worlds, between which there is no transition.

FR *What distinguishes modernity for you?*

For the United States it was the geographical, the transatlantic break with the older world, such that they consequently live in a realised utopia. From the beginning they have experienced freedom and equality as taking place, and in this sense they have been modern from the beginning. Not, therefore, that they are more technologically advanced; rather it is a matter of the principle of utopia: the United States is the utopian world. Everything that we dreamt forth here, everything unrealisable, irreal or ideal, has realised itself there, at least in spirit. Then, to be sure, one is concerned with the paradoxical situation of what to do with a realised utopia. One must not only produce it but also administer it. However, the principle is different in Europe and gives them such an immense advantage, not only technically but also mentally.

FR *Would America also be for you the land of posthistory? I believe Kojève talked about the United States and Japan as societies in which history had already disappeared.*

We can speak of posthistory because we find ourselves in history. Perhaps historical ideals are perishing today without ever actually being realised. But the Americans do not suffer from the end of history or the end of the political because they've never acted from this perspective. Perhaps they suffer today from having become a world model, in the face of which nothing is real any more. That is their crisis, while our crisis is that of impossible ideals, of dreams and phantasms. We have cultivated ideality; they have simply materialised all concepts and dreams, and they occupy themselves pragmatically with their administration. That's no postmodernity, that's radical modernity. Modernity – postmodernity, history – posthistory are for us already old problems. We have simply not radically experienced modernity. In principle, I don't know what it means to talk about the postmodern. Whether things take another course, a radical or fatal course, is more interesting than making such a patchwork with old values, which we understand as the distinguishing feature of the postmodern. But I don't have any definite view about it. Postmodern is simply a word. Perhaps the word postmodern is something postmodern and otherwise nothing.

FR *In Germany the concept of posthistory evokes great rejection, on the one hand, by those who still understand themselves to be critical intellectuals, and on the other hand it's taken up by people who believe they can use it to seize upon a social state of affairs. In Germany, the concept of posthistory was also used by theorists of a conservative derivation, for example by Spengler, Gehlen or Sedlmayr. What is this word actually supposed to say, since it also speaks about the end of history, about the social or the political?*

Actually it's only a way of speaking. Nothing comes to an end there. I prefer to interpret it differently: things surpass themselves; they do not come to an end in the sense of something existing and then no longer existing. That would be a realistic perspective, which isn't valid, because one could yet verify an end. But this isn't the case. Perhaps there was a history or a political principle, but they've become sick and tired of themselves. The space has become so full and things surpass themselves as in a hypertelic perspective. They have no meaning at all, not because they've lost their meaning, but because they have too much meaning. That means too much for all, and then they don't have any meaning any more. It is thus an intensification into emptiness or what I interpret as an ecstasy, but no condition of ending or running down. Then one sees things somewhat differently. The leitmotifs of the talk about the postmodern or posthistory suffer from too great a realism in their concepts.

FR *Lyotard staged a big exhibit in Paris, and in this connection spoke about a new sensibility that we would have to develop. Do you also see in the rapid development of information technologies and representational worlds the necessity to change our perceptive capability?*

Yes, that's an attempt to see things positively or perspectivally. It's a venture and in this sense it's good, but we don't know if it's philosophically good. Whether information is an intensified volatilisation of things, whether it's no answer to a question or brings too many answers with it and no questioning – that's a better standpoint. Then it has no consequences. One cannot interpret it as progress, not even as technological progress. The volatilisation of the old would then be more of a kind of balance, a retrospective science or technology. Perhaps that's in the sense of the postmodern, that we can panoramically condense everything with information technologies and have it all in front of us. That isn't any prospect towards a future, but the condensation of a tremendously old world. At this time, we don't know beyond this whether or not that means something else. Naturally, many things will change in the perception of things, but it isn't certain we would have more power to interpret things. We don't attain any interpretive power through informatics.

FR *But wouldn't you bring your talk about the disappearance of meaning through the surfeit of information into connection with the philosophical concept of nihilism, with Schopenhauer or Nietzsche, for example, who gave somewhat the same diagnosis without having experienced the thrust of technology?*

I hope that my standpoint isn't wistful or passive. There's always the objection that I'm so pessimistic, nihilistic or apocalyptic. I don't feel it's optimistic or pessimistic. Rather it's a question of driving logic into an overlogic, and then seeing what comes of it. People who always seek to conjure up opposing values or older values really are pessimistic; they are the really passive nihilists, as Nietzsche says. The system itself is nihilistic. We can say that in the sense that it affects itself nihilistically. But that's the situation in which we are naturally included. But when we take the process further, that's no longer nihilism. The entire hope, in so far as there is any any more, would be the leap beyond it, but in the same direction because we don't possess any counterdirection. Thus, we could take a chance.

FR *There is a book that in Germany at least has become a bestseller and was written by an American computer scientist – Hofstadter. The book is called* Gödel, Escher, Bach *and the great thesis of this book is that every system, in so far as it relates to itself – as in the Gödelian theorem – destroys itself or surpasses itself. Doesn't this resemble your strategy, where you very often describe simulation in terms of self-reference, consequently, when something is identical to itself or more real than real? The strategy of bringing self-referentiality into 'machines', of not frontally or externally attacking it, would perhaps still be the only possible subversive activity.*

Yes, that would be something like a *malin génie*, an evil, demonic spirit. When one goes at everything from the side or proceeds from a seduction of things, then everything is different.

FR *Odo Marquard, a German philosopher who comes more from the conservative corner, advanced the thesis that science and the life-world produced by it have entered the way to the fictive. That can at least be compared with what you have designated as simulation. The function science had earlier, namely to be the institution of antifiction, to stage the real, accrues to art as the modern antipode to science. Would you be able to agree with this thesis?*

That today, therefore, the real falls on the side of art? In this sense, I don't think much about art as art, as concept or as transcendence. If one has the hypothesis that everything no longer takes place in the field of production or transcendence, but in an immanence that has no outside, then there is no reason why art would not also have lost its own transcendence. It already staged this loss 150 years ago, this game with the disappearance of art. It was a very beautiful game, but today it is played out, and art is suspended in a counterconsciousness to itself, or in a bad conscience over itself. It doesn't know what it wants to do with itself any more. It can't accept transcendence, and it revolutionises itself in mere convulsions. But no alternatives arise from this. Today art is identical to all other processes. It functions like fashion or like entropic processes. I no longer see in it any brilliance or any counterforce in the real sense. Certainly there are still artists, better and worse, one can still cultivate a taste, but there's no longer any real ground for aesthetic judgement. I simply can't decree whether something is good or not any more. In itself there's no art any more than morality. It's the same simulation or immorality, or the same intensification. When transcendence intensifies, it becomes immanence. Art has played the game of intensification and transcendence; it has played out its own loss – and now it's over!

FR *Since the time of European modernity, art was the institution of the production of appearance and illusion, also of the spectacle, which you have introduced as certain anti-Cartesian categories against moder-*

nity's intention of Enlightenment, whose rationality always understood itself as disillusioning and shoved illusion off onto art. Avant-garde art has offered resistance against this arrogation and has therefore turned against itself. Doesn't your position still remain within an aesthetic perspective when you attempt to interpret the world as spectacle?

Yes, that could be, but not as an aesthetic interpretation. That's an old category. Perhaps things will collapse, no longer as aesthetic, but more brutally, for the aesthetic is still a mediating category, and the things that appear today as aesthetic appear as a simulation of the aesthetic, as an aesthetic of simulation. There is this, still. But no greater event than this can come from the realm of art.

FR *Indeed, since romanticism, the great hope was to shift into the realm of art and aesthetics in order to develop other paradigms than those of rationality.*

Naturally, the power of illusion always exists. I also insist that would be the fundamental power of illusion. But today's art has nothing to do with this power any more. It has become real or realistic, even when it's abstract or playfully postmodern. Art doesn't concern itself with its own representation, with its fashionable staging, with the incursion of illusion any more. No one really plays with illusion any more, including in the Nietzschean sense of the word. This power of illusion is lost. What it can arise from again today are objects, things, events. Pure events no longer possess the enormous heritage of art. I would sooner bet on a radical non-culture than on a new revolution in culture or art, because we already have too much history behind us. But perhaps this view comes from the heritage of Situationism. I always have something against culture as culture, against art as art, against philosophy as philosophy. Even when I talk about the collapse of the object, this is not about the object as object, otherwise there would again be a subject of something. Today's art has made itself into the subject of the game of art, and it doesn't want to end – it doesn't want to end itself.

FR *For this reason do you talk about fatality and not about beauty, which fascinates, in your concept of seduction?*

Yes, fatality or irony go beyond the aesthetic. In reality we've been concerned for a long time with a system that is beyond good and evil, beyond beautiful and ugly. And we still try to develop new categories of the old interpretation instead of playing in the radical field of the system itself. Here nothing at all aesthetic takes place.

FR *Bohrer, who for some time edited the magazine* Merkur, *maintains that in modernity art has discovered the principle of evil for itself. In* Fatal Strategies *you have likewise made the case for a principle of evil. Would you place yourself, then, in the tradition of dark writers, which constitutes a continuum of modern discourse from de Sade to Nietzsche?*

Perhaps there is such a tradition, from which I do not directly exclude myself. I have, for example, read a lot of Nietzsche. But that's not a reference in the sense of the history of ideas – rather, it's at most a connection of referencelessness. The principle of evil can be brought into modernity only paradoxically, for taken seriously it is only nonsense. It has nothing to do with a principle: rather, it's a metaphor for a twisting of things, for a perversion of things. This is how we must act today, because, in their current course, things turn so positively towards information that we must not take upon ourselves any subversion or opposing force, but rather a twisting or seduction of things. That would be a principle of evil, even if the word principle is false, but it's already a tie with an untimely tradition. Fortunately there has always been a heresy in every society, a certain dissonance, only in ours there isn't any, so there isn't any to be rediscovered. But not in the sense of a historical contradiction or a dialectic, rather as a position that's radical in the Manichaean sense.

FR *Is how one should relate to modernity a meaningful question for you? Lyotard, for example, criticises trans-avant-gardism,*[1] *as in the Italian painters and the German* Wilden, *because they relate themselves to the tradition unreflectively.*

The modern and modernity are not categories for me. For example, when I talk about the radical modernity of the United States, it is not a matter of fact, but of fiction. For me there is no real progress, only a leap into fiction. The categories 'modern' or 'traditional' are too referential. For me, the play of fiction is also essential in theory. Basically, it's all the same to me how one relates to the modern or can come to terms with modernity.

FR *So you also wouldn't defend the project of the modern, as Habermas demands in Germany?*

No, those are obsolete insights. It once made sense, but now, as Canetti says, we have already crossed this line. All rhetoric or dialectic concerning it, as if one had to make a decision about it, seems to me to be over.

FR *At the beginning you talked about the fact that one also has to accept the condition of desolation in politics. Now, in France there was the Greenpeace affair. It was obvious, at least as far as I could follow it in Germany, that French intellectuals have largely remained completely silent about it. To what do you attribute this speechlessness, which is indeed also an effect of depoliticisation? Power seems to be able to make everything immune to criticism.*

Yes, there was a kind of implicit or silent compromise between the intellectuals and the politicians, because the socialists have also absorbed and pocketed the will to speak. The intellectuals don't feel the need to say anything any more. Perhaps at this time there is stagnation in the intellectual field, but above all the will to speak has entirely disappeared.

FR *Glucksmann, for example, affirms the politics of rearmament, but the role of criticism and engagement seems to be missing.*

Yes, Glucksmann takes up the last position, perhaps to stand up for human rights, but it remains a position of reaction that sets itself against an opponent. It transpires with energy and courage, but those are old virtues. If today one no longer wants to take up a reactionary position, then there are no others, no correct ones any more. Silence is not necessarily negative, just like the silence of the masses. One must interpret it rather as suspense. The ambiguity of political power is presently so great that the intellectuals remain silent – which might also mean that today it no longer makes sense to understand oneself as an intellectual and to speak from this position. It is as nonsensical as it is arrogant. Of course, there is much to be said about Greenpeace, especially about the role of the media more than that of the secret service, which only did its job. The complicity of the media with political power was nevertheless really frightful. They didn't play their modern role, as in Watergate, for example. At present it's a wretched situation in France. But one can only interpret an event like Greenpeace as a symptom, and we're tired of merely counting off symptoms. That doesn't make sense. It was people's secret pleasure that everything is headed for a catastrophe. There was such a play of *Schadenfreude* over politics, which is perhaps not yet at an end. We don't have any illusions about the political intelligence of the socialists. No one was surprised. It was the chance for a political uproar, but it didn't happen.

FR *Is that also a symptom of the fact that political power, the stage of power, merely revolves around itself and doesn't interest anyone any more?*

Certainly this as well. What in principle takes place in this scene are not really events. They are events that draw no consequences behind them. It's amazing how it happens today. Before, governments would have fallen immediately because of it. That doesn't happen any more today because the scene is empty and desolate. No one makes anything of it, and political power has no confidence in itself, in its decisions, and the people have no confidence in the rulers. Everything runs in an empty circulation; everything works, but there's no engagement.

FR *How could one still be engaged?*

Subjectively I can't say, but I believe the others can't either. The scenario corresponds to the hypothesis of indifference. Events are merely simulated, or they aren't events any more, because everything takes place against a background of indifference. They are events of indifference. They don't mean anything any more because they don't spring from differences or power relations, but from apathy. An event like the one in the Brussels stadium would be very easy to interpret as such. It's still only a matter of upheavals against a background of indifference. If one wants to interpret everything as a play of difference, then one is mistaken. Indifference is otherwise not nothing; it isn't an emptiness, but a power. However, we can't yet interpret today what will come of it. We still don't have an interpretation for that.

Translated by Gary E. Aylesworth

NOTE

1. For example, see 'Answering the Question: What is Postmodernism?', in J.-F. Lyotard (1984), *The Postmodern Condition: A Report on Knowledge*, Manchester: Manchester University Press, pp. 71–82. [Editors]

12 On the New Technologies

Interview with Claude Thibaut (CT)

CT *From your point of view, what potential do the new technologies offer?*

I don't know much about this subject. I haven't gone beyond the fax and the automatic answering machine. I have a very hard time getting down to work on the screen because all I see there is a text in the form of an image which I have a hard time entering. With my typewriter, the text is at a distance; it is visible and I can work with it. With the screen, it's different; one has to be inside; it is possible to play with it but only if one is on the other side, and immerses oneself in it. That scares me a little, and cyberspace is not of great use to me personally.

CT *In what domains can these new technologies be used: communication, education, simulation? Are they likely to modify the attitudes and behaviour of those who use them?*

I think that it will no doubt explode in all directions, because this is a sprawling medium, and it will grow in all of the domains. But do the ends remain the same? That is doubtless the main problem. Let's take pedagogy for example: doesn't information kill education? I have friends who are experiencing this in the domain of writing, and for my part I find that their behaviour changes in a way. The possibility of indefinitely adjusting the correct version creates a sort of fantasy of perfection of the text which gives the latter another allure, another construction than those which their earlier writing possessed. The result of this quest for perfection remains problematic. We have the impression that the machine operates beyond the ends of the writing.

CT *Is there a distortion of the personality?*

Perhaps there is a distortion, but not necessarily one that will consume one's personality. It is possible that the machine can metabolise the mind.

CT *Isn't interactive communication on the Internet in particular a big novelty in the world of media?*

There is a considerable expansion of all of the possibilities, but is it a good thing in the absolute to follow through with these? Isn't there a sort of wall or overkill? Communication seems to exhaust itself in the practical function of contact, and the content seems to retreat: the network, rather than the network's protagonists, is given priority. This last becomes an end in itself.

CT *Some people seem to be excited about videoconferencing. How can this desire to see each other to communicate be explained?*

In a real face-to-face encounter, there is a complex relation, in which each person is an actor at once both present and absent. In on-screen discussion, there is only an alternating presence of one and the other. Expression is more targeted, more functional and completely disembodied. It is doubtless suitable for professional kinds of conferences. No doubt, the videoconference offers the attraction of fighting against this disembodiment. It's a way of adding to the presence.

CT *Do you think, as Monsieur Virilio does, that there are very great risks in developing the Internet?*

Monsieur Virilio is right that there is a risk of the subject being taken hostage, in a way, by his own tool. However, I do not see a doom-laden phenomenon there. I would side more with Leo Scheer, when he says that virtuality, being itself virtual, does not really happen. To make the network operate for the network by a machine whose end is to operate at all costs, is not to give it a will. One lives in the very Rousseauistic idea that there is in nature a good use for things that can and must be tried. I don't think that it is possible to find a politics of virtuality, a code of ethics of virtuality, because virtuality virtualises politics as well: there will be no politics of virtuality, because politics has become virtual; there will be no code of ethics of virtuality, because the code of ethics has become virtual, that is, there are no more references to a value system. I am not making a nostalgic note there: virtuality retranscribes everything in its space; in a way, human ends vanish into thin air in virtuality. It is not a doom-laden danger in the sense of an explosion, but rather a passage through an indefinable space, a kind of radical uncertainty. One communicates, but as far as what is said, one does not know what becomes of it. This will become so obvious that there will no longer even be any problems concerning liberty or identity. There will no longer be any way for them to arise; those problems will disappear a little below the horizon. The media neutralises everything, including, in a way, power, and virtuality itself is not able to turn itself into a political power.

CT *What do you think about the notion that Bill Gates does not have any real power?*

One could not contest that Bill Gates has material strength and a power, which appear as a form of mythology in the sense that it has no relation whatsoever with the political relation, and that it abolishes traditional structures. Furthermore, this thing is quite capable of destroying itself. The sprawling monster can develop linearly in an exponential way, then fall into a chaotic zone of turbulence leading to accident, a sort of prevention and precaution against the omnipotence of the system which turns the meanings of things upside down. Accident can appear as silent resistance, a sort of negative self-regulation of the machine. In fact, virtuality is perhaps not a universal form of life, but a singularity.

CT *Isn't this radical uncertainty brought about by virtual reality likely to challenge man's vision of himself and the world?*

Certainly, because it is the system of representation that is at issue. The image that he has of himself is virtualised. One is no longer in front of the mirror; one is in the screen, which is entirely different. One finds himself in a problematic universe, one hides in the network – that is, one is no longer anywhere. What is fascinating and exercises such an attraction is perhaps less the search for information or the thirst for knowledge than the desire to disappear, the possibility of dissolving and disappearing into the network.

CT *After all that has just been said, what about happiness?*

Happiness is essential for both the individual and the group. The possibility of having available all the means to attain it creates a kind of electronic 'high', a kind of happiness so evident that it ends up having no more *raison d'être*. There, there is a general problem of critical mass of the means which puts an end to ends. What happens when everything has been realised in modernity, when everything is virtually given? This question is crucial: where does one go from there? That is the problem: from the moment the subject is perfectly realised, it automatically becomes the object, and there is panic. I am not sure that with the virtual world we are moving closer still to happiness, because virtuality only gives possibilities virtually, while taking back the reference and the density of things, their meaning. It gives you everything, and subtly, surreptitiously it takes everything away at the same time. It is a game of which one does not know the rule[s]. One loses what one wins and vice versa. All that one can do is refuse to play, but it's not easy in our times. Books and writing will subsist in a kind of parallel existence; they will only be more precious for it because they will serve as a reference. It is difficult to oppose the virtual world because it harnesses all the polarity of the system, the positive and negative poles; it absorbs everything. One can hope that there is in each of us something singular that will allow the development of a reverted, reverting defence reflex.

Translated by Suzanne Falcone

13 I'm Not a Prophet

Interview with Michael Fordham (MF)

MF *Are you surprised at the interest of a youth culture magazine in your work?*

Yes, pleasantly surprised, but I think that a certain number of questions I raise are of a topical nature which could appeal to a younger generation. I think that there can be an affinity between an enquiry which is, on the one hand, piercing and incisive, but which is not specialised, not professional. The young generation doesn't have too much of an historical or traditional reference and I don't either. I have always tried to take a step back, to distance myself from institutions, to go beyond the institution, beyond convention, beyond the history of ideas and so on. So I think that my work can be quite easily accessed by the generations which don't necessarily have their heads full of culture.

MF *One of your most popular works focused on America as a phenomenon. What, for you, is Europe as a phenomenon?*

When I consider America, it is not in connection with Europe, in relation to Europe. I try to see it in an original, absolute light, not in relation to cyberspace but to hyperspace. I try to see it as apart from Europe. Seen from America, Europe is a bygone continent, a bit outdated, too loaded with meaning, too loaded with significance, too weighed down with culture. What I'm looking for in America is more of a free space, mentally and behaviourally. I'm looking for a kind of freedom which is much more linked to space, to territory, to distance and the relations between these things, more than a freedom of values, of political value, of philosophical value and so on. That's what Europe is, freedom understood in relation to history, politics and so on. While over there, it is a kind of freedom which is much more physical, biological, geological, really a completely different world. The book is not about a continual comparison between Europe and America. It's as if I've put myself in the same situation as those who discovered it. They arrived and asked themselves, 'What is it, this massive unknown land?' They discovered America almost anthropologically. It's because of this that I take America as a primitive society, which hasn't pleased the Americans! I approach America as a kind of virgin land, and I mean this not only physically, but mentally.

MF *Do you think that Europe is becoming like America in its collective mindset?*

Yes, but in a way it is like a parody: America really is modern, *based* on modernity or even postmodernity. I don't think that Europe can really be called 'modern'. There is always an air of nostalgia, of regret in relation to modernity here. America is the *threshold* of modernity, and that's why I say that it's the primitive society of modernity. We're an older society and no longer receptive to anything other than European history. I think that we're never going to be truly modern but we are really pseudo-modern. Europe is an area of the 'simulacra' of modernity. America is *the real thing*. We have a sort of model, a clichéd artefact of modernity. We try hard to put ourselves on the same level as America, but we don't do it very well. You can see this by all the difficulties that they are having in forming Europe as a really modern identity. There are all sorts of difficulties and it's really because all our old political, economic and social systems are still in place. We are always defending our old values. Saying this, though, I'm not objecting, I'm not necessarily for globalisation at all, but I'm saying that we want to think globally and we're not managing to.

MF *One can detect in your most recent work an increasing moralism. Is this something you're conscious of?*

I'm surprised you say that. I'm not really aware of this moralism but, yes, you could say that because when I talk about the extermination of truth, in fact the extermination of 'reality', one could suppose that this constitutes a defence of this reality. I don't think so, because I have never been *for* reality, I am more against the principles of reality and more on the side of illusion, seduction, fate and things which have nothing to do with reality. But the discourse itself is automatically moral when you expose something that has, though perhaps inaccurately, some remnants of a moral value. There exists a level of analysis which is 'beyond good and evil', if I can say that, beyond human and inhuman. Then there is a level of discourse which remains even if you're talking about truth or not. There is still the requirement of meaning that is always moral. To give meaning is a moral action. That's not a problem for me, but I resist doing it as much as possible. What I mean is that there is no moral lesson, there is no moral ideology in my work. Others, even friends like Paul Virilio, take a position which is very clearly moral, in fact almost religiously so. His analysis of the contemporary situation is very radical, while on the other hand his judgement is much more moral. Ultimately his analysis is more radical than mine, but in contrast to me I don't have any judgement like that. I know, for example, that he disagreed with what I said about the Gulf War not having taken place. 'The Gulf War is real, war is real.' It is this principle of reality which I think is the true moral principle. That's where we differ. To maintain a discourse we are forced into the *morality* of discourse, but that's the morality of communication. But that's all. Otherwise I don't think that there is morality in my work. At the same time I don't have my own ideology, personally or politically, so I'm free. Nowadays true political morality comes from existing ideologies and that's it. But I don't follow that route, so in fact mine is a radical *immorality*. That's true, I'd like that a lot, a utopia, a utopia of immorality, a discourse beyond good and evil, beyond true and false. My discourse on politics is beyond left and right, beyond distinctions – even, in a certain way, beyond morality. But I agree that we can never really achieve this.

MF *In the light of this 'morality of communication', does the Internet represent a possible new mode of communication?*

Yes, technically it's a new universe, obviously in the world of communication. It reaches for new heights, and in fact attains them. It *is* communication. I think that it is, at the same time, an extension of determination, interrelations, connection, interaction, but I don't believe in all that. I think that perhaps we can make information by travelling through communication. But, for me, the whole area has no symbolism, no symbolic intensity: it is such a technical abstraction. Communication is technical – it's not change. Change is perhaps something else psychologically, symbolically and so on. The concept of communication is sustained, *generated by technology*, so really with the Internet we attain the highest limits of communication. But what I would ask is, 'Who is it that communicates?' Who is it? There is one terminal and then another.

There are two terminals, two specific areas of abstraction which change the information. But also, all the personality changes, in fact all the charm, all these things disappear inside it. Communication is something which is factual and also artificial. In my opinion it lifts you slightly out of simulation. You are really in the field of *dissimulation*. But my opinion after the last time I used the Internet is that it is not really a place which opens up communication, an area of discovery. But I've not really had the experience, I'm not on the Internet and I don't make any use of it. However, I think it is a very powerful means of disappearance. The network is a place for disappearance and communication, data processing, cybernetics. It is the art of disappearance. What I mean is that you can immerse yourself in the machine; digitalised, virtual reality. You can immerse yourself in it and disappear completely. There are the problems of freedom, subjectivity and many others. This is something which goes round and round and round, but that's a point of view which is a little bit negative. That's true but I have the feeling that there is at least the *fantasy* of communicating. It is impossible to think that it might be possible to communicate all over the world with everyone at whatever moment in 'real time' in virtual reality . . . all that is too much. That's another utopia, a utopia which has been realised. But the danger is that utopia should not be realised because when that happens it's finished. So everyone is going to vanish into thin air on the network, but what goes on inside it? Who talks to whom? I don't feel it is a place where real events happen. It's not an original place. I'd really like the Internet to be a revolution, but it's a revolution that makes us go further into The Perfect Crime. For me it's one of the elements of The Perfect Crime.[1]

MF *Your work has tended to be viewed by academia – very often sociologists, philosophers and so on – as deliberately undermining the establishment. Is this a kind of philistinism? You have mentioned your peasant heritage . . .*

I've basically always been on the outskirts of academe, of university, of discipline, although they've treated me well. The fact that I was a little rejected by all the various disciplines is of little consequence, but it's true there was a feeling of pollution. I don't really know how to put it, but I had feelings which were 'anti-cultural', of something which was against culture. It was perhaps the peasant heritage, but you mustn't exaggerate. I may be a peasant, but at the same time I have also become a cultivated person, an intellectual. I have always refused to profit from my stature as an intellectual, or as one who is easily recognisable. There are always those who understand nothing, those who are not cultivated, the majority, what you'd call in analysis the silent majority, those who have the largest percentage of anti-cultural feelings, but not against culture in the way meant by the privileged. No. An anti-culture movement en masse has no meaning. It's the resistance to meaning, to be on the side of those who don't take any meaning, who don't see any significance, who remain removed from it. Today there are no more peasants, the peasants have disappeared, but there is still a Third World, a 'Fourth World'. Today this position, outside culture, is becoming more and more occupied by those who are excluded; by exclusion we've formed a percentage of population which has been completely abandoned, outside culture. I've always been prejudiced against culture – official culture, academic culture – and also against intelligentsia in terms of caste, the intellectual caste, the sociological casts and all that. It is this that creates a sort of privileged monopoly and it's basically this which I resist and always have. You find yourself a little bit alone, ending up forming your own caste.

MF *What are your thoughts on the millennium?*

I'm not a prophet. I feel that that we are already in a situation where we can't foresee the future. We can't make any predictions since we are already in a kind of 'real time'. There's no longer any history, any continuity, any future. Before, you could have a perspective. Nowadays, we are in an area of the instantaneous, of immediacy, of information, so we can't respond to the future because everything is here and now. We can see everything, and when we can see everything we can't *foresee* anything. I particularly have the feeling that this millennium, this 'judgement day' is not a time of communion, but more one of withdrawal. We'll arrive at the judgement day for the year 2000 with a feeling of repentance, looking backwards on everything that has happened in the twentieth century, all the violence, and so on, and there's a temptation to wipe it clean, to clean the slate: the violence, the wars, the corruption and so on. We would like to have a period of purification, purification of the century gone by. It seems to me that we kind of panic more about the final judgement day happening without our having worked out our problems because the problems are even more serious than they were before. So there's a collective feeling which is not really catastrophic. With the coming of the first millennium, people were waiting for catastrophe, though it was a catastrophic feeling which also hoped that it might be the Kingdom of Heaven arriving, so there was a messianic feeling. We have a much more negative opinion about the millennium, I think. We're not able to look to the past in order to look to the future. We are much more caught up with the present, with actuality, but an actuality which is negative, pessimistic. I haven't seen anywhere that there is any real hope for the millennium. There is more a feeling of repentance – not a despairing repentance, but still a feeling of catastrophe whether it be political, economic, ecological or even cognitive in some way. All these means of development, information, the Internet, all that, all that can give us a sense of maximum development of humanity evolved on the backs of these possibilities. It is exactly this which gives us the sense of foreboding, of upsetting everything. The image of the millennium is exactly that, that everything will be upset, that something will happen. Because in the actual world we have been waiting for a long time already and nothing has strictly happened. Yes, there are events which return to the past. The destruction of the Berlin Wall was an event, but not really an historical event. It is simply recycling history which has already happened, recycling the errors of history, and so on. So we're here and we question ourselves: we hope that something will happen, that there is an event, but we have no control over what makes an event. But, this said, this event is only for us Europeans and Americans, the Western world, because the rest of the world is not concerned at all by this millennium. You have rather a false situation because that means that the entire world has to come into line with the Western world. That's significant. That's the consecration of globalisation. In terms of time, all the continents, all the countries have to follow the Western world. At the Pompidou Centre there was a numerical clock with a countdown to the millennium. It's disappeared – they've taken it away! They say it's because of the work being done there, but I don't think so. I think they removed it because they started to ask themselves, 'What does this thing mean?' What are we waiting for? We don't know at all. The countdown is fascinating, like a show, but on one level it becomes dangerous, you feel that it becomes socially dangerous. I thought it would have been really effective, like a bomb going off at the end of the world and everything explodes. The countdown is now in the Parc de la Villette. They've put it at the back of a warehouse and it continues, but in the corner of a cellar in the dark! In place of it they've put a big noticeboard on the Eiffel Tower. It's a countdown of days, but not seconds, because that was what was worrying about the clock in front of the Pompidou Centre: there you felt some danger, but not with just days counting down. I think that we're already in the year 2000, but in my opinion it's by this anticipation that we're trying to neutralise the judgement day because it's potentially dangerous. There are no more really political events. It is the symbolic that really counts. What is clear is that all the problems which have occurred over the history of two centuries, none of them have been resolved; on the contrary, they're becoming more and more serious. Faced with all of these problems which are potentially catastrophic we are trying to go backwards, attempting to retrospectively clean up history – to correct all the errors, all the violence and so on, thereby achieving an ideal world. A utopia. To create an ideal world of communication, it's necessary that everything is going well, so we're really entering a period of *mourning*. I feel we are collectively in a period of mourning rather than having a newer, happier perspective. But that's a subjective point of view, how I feel personally. I'm not a prophet, you know!

MF *A specific question. Have you seen David Cronenberg's* Crash*?*

I haven't seen the film, but I know the novel. I wrote about it for a long time[2] and I was in contact with Ballard. I like him very much and he likes me, I think, but I didn't see the film because I enjoyed the book very much. I found it very complex and I don't think that you can put it into images. It's always simplified in the cinema. It's too visual outside of the text, even in a very hyperreal text like Ballard's. It's still complex. There are all sorts of things which you couldn't show in the cinema. I think that I prefer not to see the film.

MF *It has been very difficult to see the film in Britain. The film has caused a furore. What do you think this says about modern European culture?*

Ah, so the authorities saw the violence as contaminating? Oh, that's a very simplistic idea of contamination. I don't believe that the cinema or the TV can really be contagious. What I consider serious is the actual medium itself. It is more a virus of the actual medium, the virus of TV, the corruption of images and visuals rather than the contents which are contaminating. I don't believe contents can be contagious; the real virus is that of the medium. The complete invasion of one's mental universe just by images; everything is seen as the destiny of images. That is the true violence, that is the violence of the medium. I think that the violence of the contents is neutralised, basically, by the medium itself. You don't have to have intelligence to know that it's just TV. Like people used to say, 'It's not real', 'It's cinema', 'It's theatre', which means it's not real, but people don't say that for television. I don't think that people really believe what they see: of course there are specific cases but, as a whole, if the media really was so corrupting, a virus such as that, then the whole world would be violent, there would be nothing but violence. I don't believe that. Perhaps there is even something cathartic, a cleansing through fiction like that, through the shows that are violent. However, saying that, I am able to understand censorship for other issues, not for sex or pornography – that's normal. I don't think soft pornography is censored in Britain nowadays. On the other hand, in Ballard it is the mix of technology and sex that is specifically violent. Sex on its own isn't serious, it's the combination of the two, the 'telescopage' that, as Ballard has seen very well, is a very particular violence, and I can understand when this type of thing is banned. That seems to me a violence which is not about sex at all, it is something which is opposed to sex, something harder than sex, so it's more obscene than pure sex. It's sex mutilated by technology which has nothing to do with the sex. I don't know, I mean we have an idea of technology in the larger sense as positive. Ultimately, technology is a good thing. There are some bad points, but it can be used well and there are good things about sex and sexual liberation and so on. If you mix them together that's not using them well. That's not good at all, that's a corruption of them both. As a result of this combination, technology becomes a bad thing and so does sex. As I said I haven't seen the film, which is a pity, but I think it's in this way that Ballard has touched on something very strong; in that case I can understand censorship. It's true they should not have censored it for the reasons which they said they have, but there is something very dangerous about it, that's certainly true. I see it more as a threat for sex itself as a vital function as something everyone does, for reproduction. It is sex itself which is threatened, the sexual act. The idea of sex is replaced by artificial technology. It is the crash or the violence which takes the form of everything. There's a form of obscene pornography which sees everything as sexual and that was censored for moral reasons. What is most serious is that with this mix of technology and sex you're really starting something inhumane, no longer human. Pornography is human and therefore normal. The reasons for censorship are really very conventional, but if you take a deeper analysis you can understand why they have to censor it. Perhaps they've realised that there is really a danger of abstract violence. The crash is the absolute danger – everything's going along very well and then suddenly 'CRASH'. It is that dangerous.

MF *One final question. Today, what is your profession: are you a philosopher, are you a sociologist, are you a poet, are you a prophet?*

I can't really say. There really isn't a definition. I'm not a sociologist because the sociologists don't recognise me as one of them. I'm not a philosopher because I don't follow a history of ideas or maintain any inter-reference with other philosophers, so they don't recognise me either. What can I say? A worker, but what does that mean? No, a writer doesn't mean anything either. Thinker? But then you have the impression of Rodin's Thinker. No, I have no response. That's *your* problem!

Translated by Susanne Waddell

NOTES

1. J. Baudrillard (1996), *The Perfect Crime*, London: Verso. [Editors]
2. J. Baudrillard (1994), *Simulacra and Simulation*, Ann Arbor: University of Michigan Press, pp. 111–19. [Editors]

14 Endangered Species?

Interview with Paul Sutton (PS)

PS *The first question concerns what you said at the Institute of Contemporary Arts [London]. You were asked if you used a computer; amusing, but interesting also, because you spoke in your talk of 'automatic writing' and I wanted to know exactly what that might be and how it relates to the computer.*

Yes, it's virtuality, well, automatic writing – obviously it has nothing to do with the Surrealists; I'm not thinking of this kind of automatism of the unconscious. No, here it is the fact that the world writes itself, that it no longer exists; that the world in its presence exists only as directly coded, encoded and decoded, that it is only a matter of the substance of the code, of numeration, of accounting [*comptabilitisation*]. Inscription would be the true term really. Automatic sounds better but it's more inscription, a kind of obligatory inscription; after all everything is in inscription, in the network, and at that moment human presence, human intervention, becomes more and more superfluous, more and more pointless. Up to a certain point, machines become self-referential and the world itself, well, the processes become self-referential. It functions alone and in a certain way we are in another interspace – we don't know where exactly, we are no longer actors really, we are machine operators and, as such, we ourselves are kinds of automata. But this is not a scornful vision of automatism; it is, however, very different from the mechanical machine, that of the nineteenth century, the industrial machine – with that there is still a relationship, even if conflictual, between man and machine; there are other things, there is alienation, but there is still a duality, man/machine; even if the machine is fetishised, man exists, there is a subject and an object, whereas in automatisation there is ultimately a kind of superfusion of the two – there is no longer this opposition here. The automaton is something else; where there is no longer a subject, nothing more than a kind of object in a closed circuit, in short-circuit, and therefore the relationship is no longer the same. It is equivalent to a kind of enormous celibate machine. Mechanical machines, though, were still machines with an alterity, an otherness, whereas here it is a huge celibate machine, completely self-referential, and at this point one wonders where the real world is . . . This kind of artificial world, much more performative than ever before, completely automatised, is also an exclusion in the end, an exclusion of man, of the real world, of all referentiality. But the term 'writing', well it's really only the fact that virtuality passes through kinds of languages, numerical inscriptions, syntheses and so on. Automatic writing also interests me because of the fact that in this inscription of the world nothing can take place without having happened in its duplicate inscription. There is no simple, original or historic event really – it always happens in the virtual – it is equivalent to a kind of code of automatic disappearance from the world.

PS *On a personal level, when it comes to writing, do you find that one is too close when using a computer, that one lacks a certain distance?*

Yes, well we spoke about the fact that for me the computer is effectively . . . one is in a kind of 'real time' of writing and I don't believe in writing in 'real time'; I think that basically the computer produces a certain sort of text. I see friends who work with their computers and, I don't know, it produces a form of thinking I suppose, a sort of loop writing [*écriture en boucles*] which functions well [effectively], but which is like a program really, a kind of programming, processing; but, for me, I see writing, theory, as absolute deferral. The distance between language and the idea or between ideas and the event is necessary. There mustn't be collusion, or collision – same thing really – between the text and, well, without exaggerating this kind of confusion, between the text and the image. In other words one is entering a world where, in my opinion, the text has come into existence via the image. This leads to a lot of aesthetic performances – they have already taken place with Godard in the cinema – where the text is already also the image. It's interesting, but in terms of theory and analysis it's not possible, because there one must maintain the text as text and one must really reduce mediatisation, the technical medium really, as much as possible. And in the case of the computer, a technical medium that is extremely transparent, not authoritarian, that isn't, that doesn't seem particularly manipulative – it's not like television, and so on – in actual fact it is, in my opinion, very self-sufficient; it's the computer that works in fact . . .

PS *It's the computer, then, that drives thought?*

Yes ... in the end thought only functions when solicited by the machine or in response to questions posed by the machine itself, well by the machinic [*machinal*] logic of something like a computer. The old machines, *la mécanicité*, are not dangerous. They are alienating and correspond to a certain history, whereas *la machinalité* – I'll try and explain the difference, I don't know if it can be done in English – so, *mécanicité* is the archaeology almost of the machine and *la machinalité* is a kind of automaticity [*l'automaticité*]. It's something completely different and can be very positive. For example, I think that Andy Warhol works on the image within the *machinalité* of the image. He wanted to be a machine, a serial machine, an automatic [*machinal*] machine; so it can be positive. However in the operation of thought, to say that one cannot be, for thought, for theory, that one cannot be an operator, is not possible because with these machines one increasingly becomes an operator, so that one can do many more things. I think that it opens in fact all the mechanised possibilities, but one must not call on all of one's resources, one must never call on all one's resources. On a computer one can do anything with a text – correct it, transform it, combine it, paste it – and I feel that it's almost, if you want, the height of liberty; it's the result, the disappearance of a certain liberty, but a liberty that has no more meaning because it is simply combinatory [*combinatoire*], a sort of immense combinative liberty. But I think that for thought it's something else . . .

PS *It's a problem of excess?*

Yes, excess.

PS *What about books themselves, as actual objects, given technology such as the CD- ROM and so on?*

Well, I'm protected by the fact that I don't really have much to do with those kinds of things – it's only a tape recorder really . . . I don't even know how to use one, unless someone uses it for me, but, well I don't really have a use for one. But it's not a case of an ideological or moral refusal, you know . . . books, well that's still something, an object . . . but here it's not from nostalgia you know . . . There is a form, a rhythm in a book, you see, a kind of mental space; there is a rhythm and a physicality to the book and also a kind of metaphysicality, but difficult to express. I'm defending the book and becoming immediately anachronistic. There isn't a problem, I'm not superstitious about books or about reading. In fact I'm not an immoderate reader. Well a book is something that one can grasp, but I don't have a library and I'm not a lover of books either. A book is a mental structure [*organisation*] and there are others . . . one could propose a mental structure that no longer depended on writing which could be very good, it could be a culture – there are cultures without writing – but that's something else; we are a culture with writing. It is true that we have maintained a discursive structure of the mind which has marked us. However, whether we could, in reality, move to a non-discursive structure which would be, which would set itself up differently because there it would be of the signal, the combinatory, and so on . . . Yes, certainly one day, one day everyone will go this way I believe. Me, I might be an endangered species perhaps [*laughs*]. Well that's a choice to be made . . .

PS *In* L'échange symbolique et la mort, *it seems to me that you were suggesting that the ultimate resistance to the digital code was death. Are you searching for a position of symbolic death in relation to the proliferation of codes surrounding your work? As you have pushed various discourses, like Marxism for example, to a point of collapse, are you and have you always performed this process with your work? Is this a suicidal strategy?*

[*laughs*] Yes, it's kind of that, it's the idea of taking death to the heart of concepts or a system, where a system by definition does not carry its own death but attempts to perpetuate itself through a kind of infinite regeneration; so one must push it to the limit, evidently, where it will break down. One must take death to it – that does not necessarily mean to destroy it, it means to effectively inoculate something like the void, nothingness, death, into the heart of a system where there is none remaining. I take nothingness to the heart of the image, reinstall the void at the heart of the image. Of course everything must not be full of meaning and this seems to me to be the most vital operation, if I can say (it must be said), because when one enters into the order of unilateral production, everything is produced, and everything therefore appears as positive – OK, there is negativity but after all one is looking for everything to become positive, absolute in the world, to become subject, to become positive. This symbolic exchange between appearing and disappearing is the complete symbolic operation. Everything that appears disappears; everything that disappears can reappear – here there is a symbolic exchange. In production there is nothing finally but the moment of apparition; there is no longer disappearance, and thus we are no longer in a situation of reversibility. Disappearance in this sense is not extermination, of course; death, disappearance is no longer here, so I believe that the work of thinking is rather like this in a way, not at all fatal [*mortifère*]. It isn't an instant death, it's not that at all; it's to restore to power a kind of negativity, a symbolic form of death, a type of reversibility, to regain everything in reverse, and it is very much that that I have tried to do with ideas or with concepts like Marxism and so on.

But to go to the end of processes in order to let them disappear ... the opportunity to disappear is as important as the chance to appear. Anyway it is equivalent in a way to disappearance, the equivalent of the chance to appear, and in fact only that which has appeared can disappear; when one can no longer disappear in any way, one no longer exists. I mean that one is in a complete afterlife but one is no longer in life. It is true that our culture – modern, technical – tries to split the positive moment from the negative moment and to conserve only the positive, and so one ends up in a kind of ultrareal reality, a hyperreality which has no end. Our culture no longer contains its end – this is the problematic of *L'illusion de la fin ou La grève des événements*. That's to say that things no longer have the potential themselves for their own death, they can no longer control their own death, and that was the actual story of historical extermination in the concentration camps. The people who arrived there were not able to control their own deaths, they weren't even given the opportunity to die, they were already dead – that's extermination. One must rediscover death in a way beyond extermination or against extermination.

The word death is always open to misinterpretation, but one is forced to use such words if there aren't any others. Death here becomes a total paradigm, but it can be negativity – it can be all sorts of things – in another sense it can be the feminine, it can be, well ... it's a landmark word, symbolic, and the problem is that one cannot rewrite, or uncover all its definitions. It's an ambiguous word in a way, it carries this vast symbolic potential and the danger even of the definitive end. It seems to me that all the enterprises of a system are to put an end to death. It is a paradox, but one that is true. We are not there, but we must watch where we are going ...

PS *I'm very interested in the style of your writing – an almost excessive style, melodramatic, a hyperbolic style. Your writing seems to mirror your strategy ...*

Oh yes, I agree completely. I don't think that one can really, seriously, rigorously separate an idea from its meaning, in the way in which it is said or written. It seems impossible to me really and it is for this that I reproach writings, philosophies and so on. It is as if one wasn't taking the act of writing into account; in the end it's a medium, a way to transcribe something that might have a written meaning. Writing is a basic sense, it's a style but not really a manner – I mean that it's not a mannerism. However it is, at this point, a kind of poetic idea – the idea only exists once embodied, and that to me seems an impoverishment. My texts are always strictly about ideas and at this point it's a nihilism of this or that, it's pessimistic, demoralising, despairing, and it is never a question of the happiness of writing [*bonheur de l'écriture*]. It seems to me that writing, if one can attain it, is the happy resolution [*la résolution heureuse*] of the unhappiness of meaning [*malheur du sens*], because criticism is always unhappy by definition, whereas language is happy, you know, even when it speaks of the most desperate things – the expression can be happy and therefore still a resolution through the materiality of language and through the ambiguity of meaning or by the blockages wherein ideas are always insoluble. One will never solve the world using an ideate formula [*une formule idéeique*], by an idea; language, on the other hand, is I think a resolution, not a solution. Thought [*la pensée*] searching for absolution, a full stop, is in a way absurd. Language does not look for a solution; there are no solutions in language but there is a resolution, as in Saussure's anagrams. As for language or political language, that is the total resolution of all the elements of language that are used up. Nothing is left; the ideal situation which creates a kind of event, which is not at all an explanation of the world – evidently one can't exactly explain the world by a thought – but it is thought made world [*la pensée faite monde*]. At this point thought, the thought of language and mind [*la pensée*], becomes a sort of pure object, a pure event. It is more difficult to work with that than with a language that only wants to communicate, to transmit something. There is a kind of crime here against thought, a kind of total contempt for the very fact of writing. Someone like Barthes has clearly revealed this. He has really spoken properly of writing [*écriture*] – he seems to say: listen, you, you think; me, I write. It's an act that one cannot forget, or efface.

Thus it seems to me that in the use of a computer or word processor, writing as writing, as act, is obliterated. There is a kind of 'acting out' of writing, a kind of 'mind processing' – language is there to maintain the distance between things in order that everything is not in total confusion. So these languages exist often so that everything does not signify. Language is not just for saying anything; it's to make sure that, on the one hand, everything doesn't have the same meaning and, on the other, to make sure that things keep their distance – I don't know really if the mind keeps its distance from the world. I mean to say that language creates this distance towards the world and gives, ultimately, this impression [*effet*] of the real. Without distance, if one is the 'live' operator [*opérateur direct*] of the world in 'real time', there is no longer a need for language, it becomes a useless function, as useless as sexuality for clones; clones, once they have been cloned, no longer need to be sexualised, no longer need sex. So we are moving slowly towards the automatic disappearance of symbolic functions . . .

PS *It's more a question of a kind of information rather than the possibility of communication?*

Yes, that's it. It's all a problem of communication. Communication is no more than a sort of binary mechanism [*dispositif*] with a coder, decoder and mediator [*médium*] – well, all the functions. It must be said that semiology, semiotics and so on has in truth rendered us a great service and yet it was also extremely dangerous. There is a language of communication that can be analysed, decoded, deciphered, but the danger is to take all language for a language of communication – there is also something else in play/at stake [*en jeu*],[1] and it's an important stake because I don't believe in the magic of language. I am not a prophetic poet or anything, but in my opinion I have the impression that ideas in themselves, that is the reflexive, critical content of thought, have less and less influence in actual fact on the world. They don't in the end change much in the world. I feel that a single event of pure language is more important – not directly, it has no direct consequences, one cannot see what it becomes, what one does with it – but that existence at a given moment, through a powerful act of language, through a struggle to produce style, to give form to something, has in the long, or perhaps medium term, more importance.

So, for me, the books that I write alternate between the two; there is, however, a kind of will to communicate meaning despite everything, and besides it's true that there is a form of attraction, hyperbolic as you say, towards something other, which is of the order of seduction. There is a production of ideas nonetheless, but seduction, seduction can only come from language . . .

PS *In* La transparence du Mal: Essai sur les phénomènes extrêmes, *you talk about transaesthetics, transpolitics, transsexuality and so on. What exactly do you mean by this notion of trans? Does it relate to this notion of . . .*

No, it's not exactly transgression in the sense of Bataille, it isn't a question of prohibition/transgression. It's hard to say whether one should take a particle like 'post-' or 'trans-' or 'meta-', in which one sees all sorts of possibilities like that . . . *trans*, transpolitics, transeconomics . . . we were just saying that the economic and political processes have gone beyond their end, their finality. Transpolitics is politics from the moment when everything is political and when nothing is really political because there are no longer any real definitions – one is in the transpolitical and at this point anything that happens is no longer political and happens in opposition to the political. Thus for me this completely changes the direction of things because events, even social events and so on that are no longer interesting, happen now almost against history, against politics, whereas before they took place in the direction of history or in the direction of politics, and things changed their meaning completely according to the same events, changed meaning according to what took place in an ascendant history in the making or in a history in the unmaking which could no longer speak. Now the transpolitical is rather like history in the unmaking, because it is already beyond its own ending . . . This is the paradoxical situation, moreover, incomprehensible in a way; we are already beyond our own end, understood in the sense of finality. Production at least gave itself to a social purpose [*finalité*], historical and so on; but here, given the machinery of production, the kind of megalomania of production, excess really, but an excess completely beyond excess, production has lost its purpose, it has passed to the other side. We are no longer on this side of the end – in other words the possibility of future, utopia and so on. We have already gone past this moment and suddenly there is no more utopia and so on because everything is already behind us, and this could be the transpolitical, and one could say the same for economics, for political economy in the traditional sense with laws of equivalence, the market – all that. It still exists but it is no longer that which is determinant; above it there is a kind of space of speculation, a speculation zone, a pure circulation that is transeconomics; economics is no longer guided by rationality . . . we are in something else, in processes that are much more turbulent, uncertain, chaotic perhaps – it is here that we can also find chaos theory . . .

For the transsexual it is effectively the obliteration of sexual difference, the potential polarisation of sexuality into something that is neither exactly masculine nor feminine, or that is perhaps no longer exactly sexed, and where this sexual division of things is, at the end of the day, no longer measurable. It's not a case of going beyond the end of reproduction – sexuality already exists, it's been around for a long time, without exactly being a perversion – but the principle of sexualisation [*sexuation*], the principle of differentiation, is – here also – exceeded in a kind of automatic practice of sexuality, an automatic writing of sex, or something like that . . . with all the extra meanings that pornography (these overwhelming scenes of sexuality) and all these things bring, where sexuality . . . or desire at any rate, is effaced by its own excess, by its demonstration, its '*mise en scène*'.

So there we have the *trans*, that's what it means really. To simplify *trans*, it's that which has gone beyond its own end – perhaps it's more the transfinitive – it's a term that exists in, I don't know if it's physics or mathematics . . . the transfinitive, beyond the end, and there I think that it creates a universe where the laws, if you want, and the rules of causality and finality, are all perverted; ultimately it's a vertigo of exchange . . . The curvatures are different, we are certainly in a different dimension, but here one lacks elements of reflection to analyse this beyond of reality, not because we lack a base but because of this end of reality, this going beyond, exceeding of reality. But that's something else that we did talk about a little the other day and we could discuss at length; it's something other than the excess of Bataille where there is still a positive excess, where there is a political resolution almost, with the accursed share of this excess, where therefore there is still the possibility to restabilise, symbolically though, thanks to transgression, something . . . Whereas here we have simply passed into a sort of pure positivity, a pure virtuality . . .

PS *Where there are no longer any limits?*

Yes, exactly, and then we no longer have limits at our disposal, we no longer know where the limits are, we have gone beyond them, we have lost sight of them; it's, well, the quote I use often is that of Canetti, perhaps you have come across it in the texts, where he says that it is as if humanity has crossed, without realising it, a certain blind spot beyond which nothing is true or false – we no longer know where the limits are, and so on. And it's true that beyond limits . . . it's what produces meaning, a finality, a sense of limits and so on, beyond which phenomena become what I call extreme, extreme phenomena. That is to say that they are beyond terminism/nominalism [*exterministe*],[2] beyond their end, and at this moment they are uncontrollable – in a word, indeterminate, they are interminable. In fact they simply take the form of the catastrophe at this moment. Whereas before we were in the crisis of reality, the crisis of efficiency [*efficacité*], the crisis of values and all that, now we are in a stage of catastrophe in its literal sense. In other words, it's not exactly an apocalypse but a form of catastrophe, and we don't really have the conceptual and analytical principles to confront it . . . because all our thinking is itself formed in negativity, in criticism, in traditional analysis, which is situated between a cause and an effect, an origin and an end, [*laughs*] but here I think that there has been a sort of collapse really . . .

NOTES

1. In French *en jeu* refers both to *in play*, in the sense of boundary (the ball is still *in play*), and *at stake* (*être en jeu*, to be at stake).
2. This appears to be a neologism resulting from the conflation of the French nouns *extermination* and *terministe*. A terminist is described in the *New Shorter Oxford English Dictionary* (1993) as 'an adherent of terminism', which is defined, in the context of theology, as 'The doctrine that God has appointed a definite term or limit in the life of each individual, after which the opportunity for salvation is lost.' Terminism, in relation to philosophy, is equated with nominalism: 'The doctrine that universals or abstract concepts are mere names without any corresponding reality.'

15 Hate: A Last Sign of Life

Interview with François Ewald (FE)

FE *One of the slogans of the young people who were demonstrating last spring against the CIP*[1] *was: 'I have hate' [j'ai la haine]. It's a strange expression . . .*

Indeed, the expression is strange, for there's no object in the phrase 'I have hate'. It's the problem of these passions that no longer have an object. It's like the phrase: 'I demonstrate' [*je manifeste*], which really means I demonstrate *myself*. But for what? For whom? This is the destiny of expressions where the verb has become autonomous. They are constructed in the first person, but the object has disappeared. Take also the phrase: 'I take on' [*j'assume*]. What does he take on? He would be quite hard pressed to say. It's a subject without an object who is speaking.

FE *There's also the 'I have', as opposed to 'I am'. With a passion like hate, one* is *hate, more than one has it. From a syntactic point of view as well, the expression is curious.*

It's not exactly a syntax any more; it's a logo, a kind of label, one that, like graffiti, displays a modality of living: 'I exist', 'I live here'. Period. Within reason, or beyond all reason. Hate may be something that subsists, that outlives any definable object. Whom can one make an object of hate, today? And young people, who can they make an object of hate?

FE *It's a kind of state, a kind of modality of living, that also sounds like a condemnation. It's quite desperate.*

We mustn't overdo death or despair. They may look desperate, but I'm not sure that they are actually desperate. They might well be less desperate than others who are less disaffected. Hate is still an energy, even if it's negative or reactional. Today, there's nothing but these passions: hate, disgust, allergy, aversion, deception, nausea, repugnance, repulsion. People don't know what they want any more. People are only sure about what they don't want. The current processes are processes of rejection, of disaffection, of allergy. Hate is part of this paradigm of reactional passions, abreactional passions: I'm sorry, I don't want any. I won't join the consensus. It's not negotiable. It's not reconcilable.

FE *In the expression, 'I have hate', there's also a way of positioning oneself without demanding anything, finally. 'I have hate' is not 'I hate you'. This kind of objection parades as pure affirmation, pure position. As such, it's irrecoverable.*

Indeed, 'I have hate' is like a kind of final asset. But even so, there's a kind of alterity, someone in front of you; it can always be negotiated in one way or another, even negotiated with power.

FE *Does one encounter this type of affect in other places besides France?*

I've just returned from Australia, where my encounter with the aborigines made me experience a kind of radical anthropological shock. Alterity is truly a great problem there. The aborigines – it's the anthropological extreme, but a revealing extreme – have a kind of visceral, profound rejection of what we represent and of what we can be. As if these people also 'had hate'. There's something irremediable, irreducible in this. We can offer them all the universal charity we are capable of, try to understand them, try to love them – but there is in them a kind of radical alterity that does not want to be understood, and that will not be understood.

Between these people and the world that, since the Enlightenment, has been developed around the universal, I have the impression that the gulf is expanding. At the same time that the universal was invented, the other was discovered – the real other, precisely the one that does not fall back into the universal, the one whose singularity is insistent, even when disarmed and impotent. I have the impression that the gulf is hardening and deepening between a culture of the universal and those singularities that remain. These people cannot allow themselves offensive passions; they don't have the means for them. But contempt is still available to them. I believe that they have a profound contempt for us; they dislike us with an irreducible feeling of rejection. The young people in the *banlieues*[2] are one of the possible versions of this phenomenon – but an integrated one, whereas in the Third World what remains of all that has been destroyed or virtually exterminated holds onto a passion of radical vengeance, a kind of absolute reversion that's not about to subside.

FE *Is this current feeling of hate similar to what we used to call class hatred not so long ago?*

I don't think so. Class hatred, paradoxically, has always remained a bourgeois passion. That hate had an objective; it could be theorised and was theorised. It was formulated, one could act on it: it provided for historical and social action. There was a subject (the proletariat) and structures (the classes) and contradictions. The hate that we are talking about does not have a subject; one cannot act on it. It's only expressed by *acting out*.[3] Its modality of existence is no longer that of historical action, but that of violent, self-destructive acting out. Hate can easily turn against itself; it can also become self-hatred, self-destruction. Look at the recent suicide of the lead singer of the rock group Nirvana. He wanted to give his last album the following title: 'I hate myself and I want to die'. From now on, class hatred is part of our heritage – the European heritage, at least.

FE *In the 1980s, certain intellectuals diagnosed the end of political passions. Isn't hate a new form, the new face, of political passion?*

So we're past the end, then? Why couldn't there be political indifferentiation, now – one which would not necessarily be the last word of history, with, at a given moment, a turnaround, a hate for . . . Maybe the last drives are against history, against politics. Maybe what comprises an event is no longer constructed in the direction of history, or in the political sphere, but against them. There's a disaffection, an ennui, an indifference, which can suddenly crystallise into a more violent form, through a process of instantaneous passage to the extreme. It can accelerate as well. Indifference is not at all a quiescent sea, the flat encephalogram. Indifference is also a passion.

FE *Indifference is a passion?*

Of course. There are strategies of indifference. Indifference describes an original situation, which is not absence, or nothing. Masses, for example, are indifferent bodies, but there's mass violence, mass virulence. Indifference causes damage. The term indifference might appear flat, but it can also enter into an incandescent state. There's certainly a violence of indifference.

FE *You were speaking about* acting out *a moment ago. Isn't that a game played in the popular media? A form of passion in the television age?*

The popular media is always taken to be a kind of mirror capable of creating such special effects that what was there at the start can no longer be found. That's the most common analysis. But the forms of popular media themselves are the site of indifference; they are what produce indifference. They produce something original: the production of indifference. It's thought that power manipulates the masses through the popular media. One can also think that the reverse is true: it may be the masses who neutralise and destabilise power through the popular media. The media may be the site of inversion of rational and historical action. They paralyse and immobilise almost everything.

Obviously, the stage is occupied, it's full, but we know that nothing happens there, or virtually nothing. This is what produces the catastrophic effects. Information fills our space, but in fact the emptiness digs deeper, into a kind of black hole. Besides, do people believe in information? Everybody pretends to. There's a kind of consensus based on credulity; one pretends to believe that what happens to us through the popular media is real or true; one believes in a kind of principle of information, as a principle of divine right. But in the end, do people believe in it? I am not so sure. They're more in a state of fundamental incredulity. This incredulity is not necessarily passive. It's a resistance. It means something: we don't want that, that doesn't concern us, that's not a part of our universe. For the great majority, it's true that it doesn't relate to them, it doesn't concern them. There's a kind of enormous – not anomie, in the sense where there would be small groups of people outside the law, outside the norm; but instead a kind of anomaly, profound anomaly.

Take Paulin, the Guadeloupean man who, a few years ago, murdered those old ladies in Paris. His trial was held, he was convicted and sentenced, and he died of AIDS in prison. 'I Can't Sleep' *('J'ai pas sommeil')*, a film that tells his story, just came out. Here is a person who was absolutely monstrous – but cool, displaying no apparent hate. He was identity-less, of indeterminate gender, of an indistinct race: a kind of anticipation of a completely hybrid [*métissée*] society, a society having become perfectly indifferent. He carried out his murders without violence, without bloodshed. He was even extremely courteous, lucid, calm. He told the police about the murders with an odd detachment, a kind of indifference. One could take it to be a true indifference: someone who had become so indifferent to himself, to his own identity, that he could eliminate beings who were likewise indifferent themselves: little old men, or ladies. One might also imagine that, behind all this, there's a core of radical hate. Paulin may have had hate, but he was too stylised, too cultivated to express it in a violent way. That hypothesis is also possible.

FE *Can one say that hate has become our dominant political passion?*

Communication, in becoming universal, has been accompanied by a fantastic loss of alterity. There's no more other. Perhaps people are searching for a radical alterity, and hate, a desperate form of the production of the other, may be the best way to make it appear – as well as the best way to exorcise it. In this sense, hate would be a passion, in the form of provocation, of defiance. Hate is something strong; it must provoke a sharp adversity, and our world hardly provokes adversity any more, because conflicts are immediately shut off, circumscribed, invisible. Hate is an ambivalent sentiment that can be inverted. It's a much stronger way of relating than love, affection, consensus or conviviality, which are the weak modes of communication.

FE *One cannot avoid comparing the present situation to the 1970s, when people were talking about 'peace and love' all the time. It was the era of resistance to the Vietnam War, beatniks, hippies, 'sous les pavés la plage',*[4] *John Lennon's 'Imagine'. There was so much love everywhere that finding a way to love power became a big question.*

It's true that at that time everything revolved around the libido, desire and libido, things that curiously have weakened considerably since then, except in advertising. As to power: where is it? No one is able to capture power any more, even to fight against it. Hate is no longer class hatred, since it no longer sets the rich in opposition to the poor, the bosses against the workers. It's a hate for the class of politicians, an aversion for the political class, a global hate that has found a way to express itself in various political scandals, without being reduced to them.

FE *Can one say that this hate comes at the end of history? Is it the passion that accompanies what Francis Fukuyama has described as the end of history?*[5]

I was just in Frankfurt with Francis Fukuyama, actually. I told him he was optimistic talking about the end of history. That would mean that history has taken place, that it's finished; it would suppose that there was history. Ultimately, there's more of a kind of passage beyond, beyond an interminable history. Hate is more the violent reaction to the fact that there's no solution, that there's no possible resolution to all the problems posed by history. It's a rejection of the course of history; it's a kind of loop, a regression, one doesn't know what one is dealing with. Perhaps, beyond the end, in these border regions where things are inverted, it's possible that there's an indeterminate passion – one which necessarily would not be a positive one, in the way that love is positive. Whatever energy remained would be inverted in a negative passion, a rejection, a repulsion. Identity today is found through rejection; it hardly has any positive base any more. All that remains now is self-anti-determination, more through the expulsion of the other than by relation or affective dialectic. This is a situation which is becoming jammed. Certainly, there has been a kind of rupture that has not really been perceived. We've been swinging back and forth, not in a kind of positivity of time, a linearity of time any longer, but in a kind of countdown. Take the numeric clock at Beaubourg:[6] it testifies to the fact that we are in an odd temporality, no longer in a time which is counted up from the origin, and increasing – but instead in a countdown. The end is there, and there's nothing else to do but count what separates us from it. Counting from the end, it's truly an odd perspective; it obviously is not done in order to increase our positive passions.

FE *What politics is possible in the age of hate?*

Rediscovering political passions: such is the great desperate hope of intellectuals. There have to be stakes in politics again. I believe that the true passion, the fundamental passion, is that of the game; it's the one which overdetermines all the others. When you play, you are impassioned. If you play, if there are stakes, then there's a passion, neither positive nor negative – a passion of battle that expends itself. You play, you lose, you win. It's not a question of progressing; whatever you win you lose right back, and so on. Passions come from there. In contemporary politics, where are the stakes? They have been shut off, there's nothing but stakes in this or that category, corporate stakes. It's as if there's an impossibility of putting something at stake. Thus, there's no more passion in politics. There's only an apathy, and on the other side – to play on words – a compassion. We are no longer in impassioned politics; we are in compassion, through the extension of human rights, of solidarity.

FE *The humanitarian?*

There's a sort of radical dilution of passion into a sort of compassion, which Hannah Arendt analysed and criticised long ago when she explained that, with the Revolution, the compassion for the happiness (and especially for the unhappiness) of others took the place of passion, of freedom, of action – which are politics proper. We've fallen into the consensual universal of human rights, which conceals and nourishes violent singularities that secrete hate precisely to the degree that this universal is inadmissible – it's a utopia that can reveal itself to be murderous. It begins in enthusiasm, but when a system truly arrives to the point of the universal, to the point of saturation, it produces a terrible reversion, and all the accidents we're seeing now, in the form of virulence, which has in a way replaced historical violence. From now on, we will have to deal with anomalous systems that secrete all sorts of virulence: AIDS, computer viruses and so on. Hate may also be a virus of this kind. Perhaps hate is vital, vital in the sense that it's the worst thing that can happen if you have no enemies any more, no more adversity, no more antagonism, even virtual antagonism. If you take away hate's natural predators, it destroys itself. There's a vital metastability, a kind of equilibrium that implies that there's an other, and an evil, enemy other. If you don't have to defend yourself any more, you end up destroying yourself. This is what I have called *depredation* – depredation in the sense that the predators have been removed. Hate may also be a last sign of life.

FE *It's said that hate is nationalist, and that nationalism is hateful. What do you think of current analyses of the return of nationalism?*

They're superficial, and overly moralising. The analysis should be a bit harder, tougher, and it shouldn't immediately short-circuit phenomena with value judgements: this is not good, Le Pen or Islam shouldn't exist. It's not necessary to call for a return of human rights, since it's precisely that culture of universal values that secretes the current state of things.

FE *Is there a danger in the universalism of human rights?*

One doesn't need psychoanalysis to know that a human being is an ambiguous animal, that one cannot root the evil out of him, or simplify him to the point that he would be no more than a positive and rational being. Yet, it's upon this improbability that the ideologies rest. It's necessary to have adversity, incompatibilities, antagonisms, things that are irreconcilable, at the risk that the most sordid passions might be revealed. There's no choice. It's necessary to work with these things.

Modern politics begins with the will to dialecticise, to equilibrate forces, to find strategies of compromise between things, which are always thought to be negotiable. The principle of modern politics is that nothing should be able to evade this enterprise of reconciliation and negotiation. If there has to be conflict, it's meant to be resolved. Modern politics includes a final solution principle, which leads sometimes to 'the' final solution. This is the dialectic. But reality is not dialectical; it's made up of irreconcilabilities, truly antagonistic things, as Freud posited Eros and Thanatos to be: radically mutually exclusive, and absolutely irreconcilable even to an infinite degree. Other cultures know how to manage this fundamental ambiguity – symbolically, through the use of sacrifice, of rituals, of the ceremonial. But we don't want to take it into account. We start with the principle that things must become clear, become transparent. At the same time, there's a residue that's not dealt with, because it cannot be dealt with; it becomes necessarily residual and negative, and transforms itself naturally into hate. In pushing the universal as far as it will go, as we have done, this necessarily provokes a reversibility of these things, and other singularities will be provoked in turn. I am not a pessimist; the singularities are indestructible.

FE *Can hate be universalised? Can one imagine a federation of hates? That the* banlieues *might make links with various nationalisms, which themselves might make links with something else, in a sort of International of hate?*

One would almost wish for such a scenario to be implemented. But by definition, what is inertia, indifference, cannot be put into solidarity, since it's an effect of the breaking up of solidarities, an effect of the failure of the universal. It's fractal, fragmented, it erupts here or there, without the optimistic possibility of finding a political coherence. No, the worst is not always possible.

If there had to be a linkage, it would be of the order of a chain reaction, which is the current way in which events are propagated. Not through information any more, nor knowledge, nor reason, with its reasoned and reasonable progressivism. There are trigger moments, uncontrollable linkages, like those described by Elias Canetti in *Crowds and Power*. The mass is a dull type of body, but transmission in it is ultra-rapid, through an effect that remains mysterious to traditional sociological analysis. Fashion is a kind of ultra-rapid contagion. It's the virulence of the virus, but not all viruses have perverse negative effects; some of them have perverse positive effects. We're in a universe of ultra-reaction, of overreaction, of chain reaction, of immediate contiguity. This is the modality of the popular media today, the modality of communication. Obviously, in a universe of this kind, political action is much more difficult.

FE *Traditionally, political philosophy starts from the principle of a self-conservation which resists the dangers that threaten the individual. Today, with people like André Glucksmann, one seeks to base a morality on the recognition of a principle of radical evil – in a certain way, then, through a sort of hate of all evil. Could hate be the principle of a new morality?*

I have nothing against evil, the principle of evil. With evil, it seems to me, there's an active principle, on the condition that one doesn't demonise evil, that one doesn't pathologise it, as Glucksmann does. There were all those analyses, in Bataille for example, according to which the energy of societies comes from the principle of evil, not from their positive passions but from their negative ones. This is also what I've called the transparence of evil: evil is no longer played out, it no longer plays a part. It moves elsewhere, and appears transparent everywhere. Instead of being graspable, it becomes ungraspable. It takes the form of all these viruses that worry us today. But does that mean we need to use a demonic principle?

FE *Isn't there a little of all that in Nietzsche? The idea that it's also necessary to know how to hate?*

It's necessary to be ruthless: you have to push everything that is leaning, so it falls. That's the strategy of the very worst, upping the ante, a passage beyond. I like that logic very much. It's necessary to know how to go to extremes. The problem is that more often we fall short of good and evil. We've lost the values, and the standard opposition of values – not by passing beyond them, but in falling short of them. From now on, values will be indiscernible, they will be undecidable, they will drift.

The good is when there's a managed opposition of good and evil. The good completely admits the existence of evil, but says that there's a possibility of reconciliation. All our religions, our ideologies start from the principle of good. Evil is when there's no more possible reconciliation between good and evil, when the two poles are torn apart. We are thus now within evil, in the sense of irreconcilability, which is inadmissible from a moral point of view. Evil means that there's no possible reconciliation between the two.

FE *That doesn't give much of a future to our present politics of integration.*

It's true that, until the middle of the 1980s, in our cultures, the process had not been going in the direction of exclusion. That has changed. Now, something completely evades social regulation. Even if it's not the end of history, it's certainly the end of the social. Something has been dissociated; a principle of dissociation is at work, and there's no end in sight.

We are no longer in anomie, but instead in anomaly. Anomie was quite pleasant. Anomie arises in a bourgeois society. Anomie is that which, through a temporary exception, is not within the law, but which one hopes to re-inscribe within the law, to put it back on the right track, through solidarity. As for anomaly, it's irrecuperable. It's not about light disturbances. Anomaly is not what evades the law, according to some rule of evasion. It's more profound: the rules of the game are not necessarily articulated. No one is necessarily supposed to know them. One might not know anything about them; yet one knows that people avoid the game completely, escape the possibility of playing the rules of the game. The law is explicit, one can contest it, and anomie provided a principle of resistance, of subversion, whereas anomaly is completely irrational; it's what falls elsewhere, what cannot be played out any more, what's no longer in the game, what's outside of the game. One doesn't know what's fomented there, in anomaly.

FE *Can anomaly have hate as a passion?*

Perhaps we live in a general process of the reversion of things – a process that would be augmented by various passions, like hate. Without knowing it, we would have passed to the other side, we would have moved into systems which are more and more sophisticated, functional, operational, and at the same time more and more threatened by a breakdown, by a violent reversion. It may well be that this is the very problem of the species itself, and not only the problem of certain cultures that might be trapped in a process of self-destruction. We've already seen cultures collapse like that, in one fell swoop, without knowing why.

FE *We're all Incas, then . . .*

One doesn't have to go so far: just look at communism.

Translated by Brent Edwards

NOTES

1. CIP: *Contrat d'Insertion Professionnelle.* Contract offered by the French government to unemployed youth, guaranteeing them a job for an inferior salary.
2. The *banlieues* are the often impoverished suburbs around many of the large cities in France.
3. In English in the original.
4. '*Sous les pavés la plage*' ['Under the paving stones, the beach'] is a catchphrase coined during the student demonstrations in Paris in May 1968, strongly associated in France with a romanticised memory of that period. When protestors removed paving stones from the streets to build barricades against the police, they were surprised to discover that the underlying soil was yellow and grainy, not unlike beach sand.
5. See F. Fukuyama (1992), *The End of History and the Last Man*, New York: Free Press.
6. Outside the Pompidou Centre at Beaubourg in Paris there was a large digital 'clock' which counted down the number of seconds remaining until the millennium.

16 Europe, Globalisation and the Destiny of Culture

Interview with Monica Sassatelli (MS)

MS *Do you think it is possible to talk, as people increasingly do, of a European identity?*

I think that originally Europe was an idea. The true European identity was an idea, a dream even, a utopia. Europe existed perhaps more as a circulation of ideas in the Middle Ages than today. This idea today has become true through economic, political, structural means; in this sense it is already achieved, there are no problems, it works very well. It works very well on the market side, that is, the side of globalisation, of which Europe is just a micro-model. Frankly, I do not believe much in this Europe. In considering European identity, first of all it is to be stressed that identity itself is a utopia. It is where one takes refuge when there is nothing else left to do. Until there was prestige, glory and culture there was no need to tell oneself: 'I am this, here is my identity, I exist, I am here.' When one truly exists because there is strength and glory, at base, there is no need for identity. Identity is a weak value, a refuge value somehow. Today it is on this that Europe is being built.

I have an example. A few years ago I was in Venice at a meeting on European cultural identity. It could be felt that the Europeans were not at all convinced, they did not know what they were, they could not identify themselves. On the contrary, for Borges, the Argentinean, Europe really existed – he knew what it was, because it was a powerful idea [*idée force*]. The same applied to the Eastern European countries: they could see Europe because they wanted it, desired it, whereas Western Europeans had no real European desire.

MS *One could argue that you have written a book on Europe with your essay entitled* America. *In it, the Other of America is consistently European, and almost never French, Italian, English: 'we' is European.*

It is contradictory actually. Europe wants at the same time to be the exception, the European exception to globalisation – France in particular – and a kind of global power, that would counterbalance the United States, rival the United States. There is thus a total ambiguity. Europe can try to reactivate its old values (we always repeat: we have history, others have no history), but I don't really know what can be reinvented from that. However, I don't think that the question stands in terms of identity. Americans, for instance, do not problematise their identity. They are American, that's it.

MS *In* America, *Europe's image emerges as something opposing globalisation and its peculiar characters. One would almost say that all the elements that you have described elsewhere as characterising the contemporary world – simulations, the hyperreal and so on – have come true only in America. The contrast delineates a vision of Europe that is even romantic, a romantic modernity, described without nostalgia but infinitely distant from the world of simulations and the hyperreal – a vision that I think can be found only in this text.*

Yes. It is easy to notice, in France for instance, how identity is always constructed against America, as a countermodel of America. There's a confusion to underline here. America is confused with globalisation, while America is as much a victim of globalisation as any other country. The world is the locus of globalisation. In this framework, it seems that Europe – and France as a particular case – is a kind of by-product, a derived product of globalisation. As usual, Europe follows the same path as America, but always with a serious delay in terms of modernity – always twenty or more years behind – and the American model is never attained, a model that has at least the merit of originality. The American model is the real place, or non-place evidently, of globalisation, but it is not its subject or its agent; there is no strategy of globalisation, it develops irresistibly. However, the confusion is also at another level: not only between America and globalisation, but also between globalisation and the concept of the market. Now, that seems to me something totally different . . .

MS *How do you see the relationship between this Europe as an idea, as a cultural space, and institutional Europe, the European Union?*

I do not have much of a sense of institutions, I distrust them. With regard to Europe, I have the impression that this is a kind of substitution, the creation of Europe in virtual terms. The perfect example is the Euro. Europe has not been set up as a federation, but there is a common currency, against the will of practically every country. There is a common currency, an artefact that it is hoped will lead to the creation of a political Europe. But I do not think so. Europe still does not exist, but the European currency does. Or, better, Europe exists in institutional terms at the summit, but nothing assures that there will be no ups and downs, accidents; nothing guarantees that Germany will not one day say 'I withdraw, I take back the Mark' . . .

MS *Indeed, in the European treaties there is no such possibility.*

Absolutely. But you never know, because it is clear that it is the doing of what is called the European technocracy. Now I don't want to be populist, but it is clear that the peoples, as they say, basically are not European. Even in France the referendum on Europe was practically fifty–fifty, and today it would probably fail. It is a completely schizophrenic situation, something that exists in a kind of hyperspace, hyperreality.

MS *As you write in* America, *universality is one of the characters of European culture (and French culture in particular). However, it is precisely universality, having crystallised within nations, that hinders the federation of Europe. It is the history of nations and their cultures that causes contemporary difficulties in finding, as you wrote, a 'European dynamism' [*élan européen*]. Could you develop this? Do you think this is as true today as when you wrote* America *in the eighties?*

Yes, in a way. I have always seen three levels: the nation, between originary particularities [*singularités originelles*] and the universal dimension. Nations have been produced on a reduction of singularities: it was necessary to reduce all differences in order to make, for instance, France. Originary particularities have been reduced to an abstraction, the nation. And nations are also contemporary with the abstract idea of universality, the idea of the eighteenth-century Enlightenment. All this was born at the same time; therefore the universal has been created in some sense by Europe, not the feudal Europe of singularities, but the Europe of Enlightenment, humanist Europe, Europe of national bourgeoisie.

Now, as an idea the universal is opposed to that of the global. Universal values can resist the global. But today they only exist in a ghost-like manner, if I can say so, like human rights. It is clear that today the so-called universal values succumb to this other thing that is the global. The global destroys the universal as an idea and destroys all particularities, at a global level, not only European. It is a double task of reduction. The question then is: should we fight for the universal against the global, or for the particularities? I have the impression that the universal is annulled, and today the real fight is between the global – a kind of abstract global power – and all the particularities that revive, but in an uncontrolled state, sometimes even as racism, nationalism – religious, ethnic, linguistic – that globalisation will provoke more and more. Between the two, universal values, including national values as they existed in the golden age of nationalism, abate. Europe will be, at the same time, the place of a transnational pseudo-federation, and increasingly of greater re-particularisation, that is, of a dispersion, a kind of diffraction. Perhaps there will be no more nations. There will be great regions, some rich and some poor, of course. That is, the contrary of harmonisation: greater and greater discrimination. My outlook is not rosy.

MS *However, European institutions appeal more and more to common cultural elements to promote the creation, or the awakening, of a European consciousness.*

Yes, it is so, but I do not know how it will develop. To unify a conscience is to create an identity; identity is the unification of a conscience. If we take America, there has never been unification. There is a great autonomy of the states, even individuals have a great autonomy towards institutions, and that happens in an uncontrolled way. It is maybe harder, but it is like that, and develops a far greater energy than this kind of grass-roots democratisation that we try to make in Europe.

Moreover, the question is in terms of culture – now, today, what is culture if not the substitute for a political identity not to be found? As political energy, political reality dissociates and cannot be found; culture substitutes for it. Culture becomes a kind of plasma that everybody can access democratically and share. Now I do not think that real culture is something democratic that can be shared in whatever way, in the multimedia for instance. That is hyperculture, that will clearly be the place, the abstract space–time of a utopia in which, through culture, the political can be reached, whereas in reality culture replaces absent politics. Therefore, that will not lead to politics. There will be a kind of cultural multidimension, as there is a financial dimension, an economic dimension; there will be a market of culture as there is a market of shares, of the stock exchange.

MS *Recently, the European Union introduced various symbolic measures, choosing for instance a flag and an anthem. These are means that at the national level seem to have lost some of their importance. Also, in this case America seems to be an exception: in America the flag is everywhere. You have also pointed out that the American flag has become a kind of corporate logo, more than a symbol. Could we say something similar for the European flag?*

Yes. An enterprise needs advertisement, a logo, labels. Everything happens at the level of signs, as in a kind of magic, as if signs make the thing exist. This is part of a kind of intoxication, of commercial manipulation. It is not a spontaneous outburst. No, it is really like a business, and also Europe is now managed like a business, with managers, in Brussels.

Even if a political Europe was created, if it had its own identity, different from America, the fact would remain that at the financial and commercial level Europe does not exist in itself, finance will always be international. It is a long while since finance recognised Europe. Europe is only a very small part of it. Even if a political, identitarian Europe existed, economy would function globally. Therefore this political Europe would not even be autonomous, maybe not even in cultural terms. Whatever you do, you have to deal with powers that are internationalised, that have not waited for the idea of Europe to internationalise – they are so from birth. Capital is international, not European. Today we speak of a global economy, of global networks, and countries look for any kind of protectionist measure to recreate a kind of artificial autonomy. It is very interesting, and ambiguous.

MS *In* America, *you also describe European specificity, by comparison to the United States, in terms of taste.*[1] *Could a 'community of taste' have a role in the formation of European identity?*

I don't know. Taste belongs to the realm of sensation, of aesthetics. Could it have a role for Europe? Does a community of taste exist? I am a bit doubtful, because taste is so subjective. But I have the impression that many aspects of taste have today become a matter of fashion, which is transnational, internationalised. Also taste is at risk, but maybe it is true that taste resists better. There are things that resist better. Language for instance, I think language resists. And taste as well, but one has to specify what is meant by it: taste in the sense of custom resists well, even if Brussels is trying to destroy French cheese! Aesthetic taste has become collective, therefore it is a difficult question. In America the problem of taste almost does not exist any more – one does not ask if there is or there isn't taste. It is a term that is not part of modern culture. Taste and colours – nowadays they seem to me more and more planned, but this is banal. An authentic right to taste and colour should be invented . . .

MS *Identity is not an important issue only for European institutions. Many authors, and you among them, have underlined the contemporary obsession with identity. Do you think that this obsession may be linked to culture's becoming a kind of stock of empty symbols, as you maintain for instance in* Symbolic Exchange and Death?

Yes, maybe. Inasmuch as there has been an attempt at juxtaposing all cultures, let them communicate – culture today is communication – according to me this is a total degradation of culture. It is difficult to define culture, but in what we may call the anthropological sense it is something singular. Culture is a singularity. It is like languages: every language has its own universe, its symbolic universe that is incomparable, non-exchangeable. But the culture with which we deal today is like inventing a universal abstract language – and it is being invented already, it is the artificial languages, numeric languages – then culture is really becoming a kind of lowest common denominator. It is reduced to its simple elements, then recomposed. It is a synthesised product. It is as such, as synthesised product, that it becomes universal.

There has been a beautiful moment of culture, not only singular but universal culture; actually, it is between the seventeenth and the nineteenth centuries again. Here we find exchange, cultures bump into each other, and considering also the irruption of primitive cultures, it is a very interesting moment. But today, with globalisation, all differences are annulled, or else it is a game of differences, but there is no longer a real clash, an alterity of cultures. Now, cultures are rivals, they should not be reconciled, it is not possible to reconcile cultures, it is not possible to reconcile languages. They are really incompatible, and sometimes antagonist, rivalries. Exchange need not be impossible. There can be relations, but only if each culture preserves its own specificity. I can understand that people fight for their culture, to defend their language. I understand it, even for currency. In fact, I do not understand why people do not fight more for currency, because symbolically (not in economic terms, but symbolic) it is very important.

Now, inside Europe, conceived of as distinguished from globalisation, the attempt is to create this kind of common platform, in which everyone will be forced to accept common legislation: it is this that creates more and more resistance. The more this process advances, the stronger resistance becomes. Then the problem of identity is increasingly central. But there can't be identity without alterity; if there is no other, there is no self. Today one does not know where the other is, because with globalisation there is no other. I have the impression that we are leading to an impasse. It is impossible to forecast what will happen, but it is possible to see that there are zones of resistance.

Also, the distinction between the elite – the technocrats, those who are in power, who invent this abstract generality, who manage things – and the others should be considered. There really is an increasing gap. It is known that the leaders of all countries will want to be integrated in Europe. At some point all of Africa will want to join in Europe. It is fantastic – but totally idiotic. This is the project of an elite, not in a qualitative sense, let's say of a minority that manages things, that has all the means to make them happen. Therefore there will be Europe, but it will be a kind of pseudo-political event; in reality, deeply, politically, nothing will happen. I even think that compared with the idea of Europe that emerged in the fifties this concretisation is more of a scattering.

MS *Is it possible to relate your thesis that signs have become empty, without a referent, to the idea of a different balance between power and symbolic exchange? In other words, if institutions today give less, as they give only signs, images, does this give the individual a chance to be less in debt?*

It is an interesting question. Is it possible to think of being less in debt? Maybe. But it has to be said that a sign in general is not 'less'! It is not less than a thing, as if a sign weighed less than a thing, was more volatile. No, today in a society like ours the sign is everything, as it substitutes the real, the referent. Therefore signs, like information and all immaterial things that we are given, are more important than the redistribution of material goods. I do not know whether this dematerialisation lightens the debt. It is possible to consider it starting from incredulity. It is true that there are signs, but are we bound to believe in them? It is not certain at all. And if you do not believe, you somehow also refuse the obligation to be bound by whatever debt. Therefore in that sense there is a kind of lightness, of volatility towards all that comes from authorities – media, political. There is a kind of fluctuating irresponsibility that is everywhere, it is true.

MS *In other words, on the one side one cannot escape from signs because they are everywhere, but on the other they do not impose an interpretation.*

Yes. And moreover signs come from everywhere and nowhere. There is no longer an origin, a source. In symbolic exchange there is always a properly dual relationship, therefore there is real responsibility, debt, obligation. Whereas now there is a kind of mediasphere, hypersphere, from which things come and with which one does not feel in a dual relationship. It would be impossible anyway, as there is no alterity. We have therefore to deal with a strange hyperreality. Maybe this is one of the causes of collective depression, because it is very difficult not knowing to whom one should answer. Not knowing of what to answer and to whom, and therefore suddenly not being identifiable any more. When there is oppression, when somebody is oppressing us, we know what we have to deal with; we can fight. When someone gives something, when there is a giving power, we know to whom we are indebted. Before, there was religion, there was God for this, it was perfect, one could give thanks to God. Today, no, there is no one to thank. Therefore the situation is disequilibrated.

One can recall the European question here. Brussels is such an abstract place, it is not to Brussels that one is going to feel in debt. No one will feel a relation of reciprocity, of obligation, of responsibility towards Brussels. It is a curious deconnection [*déconnection*]: something works like this, in orbit, but nothing changes here. It is a strange situation.

MS *Often, also in this interview, you have framed the question of the relationship with institutions, with globalisation, with the 'mediasphere', with the excess of signs, in terms of resistance. What, then, is the connection between resistance and distance, emptiness? If we take seriously the remark that today signs come to us empty of content, of meaning, is it possible to see in this very emptiness an occasion for resistance? Is it possible to find in the medium as such, as empty of content, a prompt for resistance?*

Yes, it is true. I think that actually the lack of meaning, to be insignificant or non-significant is ambivalent. It can be very negative, a real loss – the lost object – or on the contrary can be the base for a strategy. It is true that the system with the pre-eminence of the medium creates such a situation, that can then maybe be exploited, maintaining the idea that meaning is lost. I think for instance of political language. It is a language that has no meaning, beyond meaning, but which works with the immateriality of language, with pure language. You can turn its absurdity against it. There has been the idea of turning the medium against itself, of making of it an excessive use for instance, a delirious use. This strategy has been used by Americans in the sixties, the seventies. To fight against the media on the grounds of the media, to exceed them, to go further with the same logic.

I'm thinking of photography, because it is what has interested me more. One can see in it an altogether different idea of technique, of technique as medium precisely. In photography, in the photographic act, what is interesting is that even the object disappears, along with the subject. Technique functions as a medium of disappearance, but also as the art of disappearance. So in this case it is not negative at all, on the contrary. Technique puts an end to the unilateral mastery of the subject over the world. Technique, which should work for our hegemony on the world, on objects, works in reverse in that the object appears through the technique. It is the object that in some sense uses technique, clandestinely, secretly, ambiguously, in order to appear, to exist. Then, I would be cautious, but one could restate the question of technique in these terms.

MS *One could remark at this point, banally if you like, that you still need to presuppose the existence of something, of a subject, that orients technique towards the better or worse result . . .*

Yes. But there is a point in which the autonomy of the medium, the fact that it is the medium that acts, is important. Certainly there is always the subject. We can take as an example the computer: all the operations are programmed by a subject, somewhere they have been thought of by a subject. But at a certain point in the technical act the subject itself gets lost, loses its identity, its mastery. Something happens that it is no longer in the mastery of the subject.

MS *Coming back to symbols and images: you have often referred to the concept of the aestheticisation of everyday life. It seems to me that such a concept, as it is commonly described, amounts to a kind of anaesthetisation, obfuscation of the senses, which hinders the reaction to stimulations.*

In fact the way in which aestheticisation is described seems rather anaesthetising. But, otherwise what is aestheticisation? The aesthetic is ambiguous today, as is economy. This general aestheticisation is a levelling, a neutralisation. Whereas if you take aestheticisation in the strong sense, then there is distance, there is an aesthetic judgement. There is pleasure also – this is what is being threatened. Is it possible to find it again? Yes, I hope so, but today the risk is to fall back into aesthetic models, and therefore into an aesthetics that is no longer about subjective taste, subjective judgement, but about models. Hence distance is lost, and only a play of model and countermodel is left. One is really dealing with a kind of cultural cloning, of aesthetic cloning too. Today this extension of culture implies a kind of general extension of aesthetic banality. It is part of political correctness, so to speak. Enterprises give themselves a wealth of signs, identification marks, promote culture. The great risk today is this type of aestheticisation. They say: all becomes market, economy, value, all becomes commodity, aesthetics included. I would say instead that the main risk is, on the contrary, that all today's commodities are aestheticised: it is a kind of cultural aesthetic legitimacy, and that is the real globalisation.

All this does not offer many possibilities for rediscovering a dimension of distance, a dimension that would really create another scenario. As long as there was the real – if we can say so – there was the imaginary as well, as there was the possibility of aesthetic distance and of aesthetic sublimation. In the hyperreal it is much more difficult because the real swallows the imaginary as well. In the hyperreal everything is actualised, therefore distance is more difficult to find. Is it possible to oppose this new violence, invisible, imperceptible, to contest it, question it by recreating a violence of the traditional type in some way? Is a defence in the name of ancient values possible? Can resistance come from humanistic values, the values of the Enlightenment, or else should something more radical be invented? I would be for the more radical way.

Then resistance would not be precisely aesthetic. When I say rediscovering particularity, it is no longer in the aesthetic realm. When I talk of photography in this sense, an image that would really be an image, it is no longer on the aesthetic plane, nor on the moral plane. It is about objects, or situations that would be beyond good and evil, but also beyond beautiful and ugly, transaesthetic, that overtake the system from above, going further somehow, but considering objective conditions, rather than trying to rediscover a defensive strategy reactivating aesthetic values.

MS *But if we recuperate the etymological sense of aesthetic, therefore sense, sensation, could this notion bring a dimension of resistance,*

resistance precisely to the anaesthetised state brought about by the surplus of stimulations?

Re-sensitise things, give them a sensitive side again. We are not talking of art at this point, it is really the level of sensations. Yes, maybe I agree, on the idea of reinventing a body, sensations, sentiments. To reinvent sensation as passion somehow, *aisthesis*, the aesthetic of the sensible, and not of the sensational!

NOTE

1. J. Baudrillard (1988), *America*, London: Verso, pp. 74–105. [Editors]

17 Between Difference and Singularity

This open discussion took place in June 2002, and followed Baudrillard's reading of his text, 'The Global and the Universal'.[1] The discussion was facilitated by Wolfgang Schirmacher (WS) and Friedrich Ulfers (FU).

WS *This is the bad news. What is the good news? Many of your questions have to do with 'is there anything positive?'*

It's very optimistic.

WS *He uses the Heidegger defence, 'I don't want to criticise, only to describe!'*

Audience *I liked your comment about the Ministry of Culture as being a kind of joke. I think the situation is very well typified by the fact that the Ministry of Culture is required to subsidise cultural production. However, cultural production in its best forms can be stockpiled. It's not perishable, it doesn't have to be consumed at once. At a certain point you say it's simply illogical to say that we won't be saturated by cultural products. My point is, I think that cultural products can be stockpiled without perishing. What is the difference between cultural products and market products?*

It would be a fantasy to cryogenise culture, in order to resurrect it in a hundred years, like Disney in his cryogenic grave. Why not do the same with human beings? They are about to become consumer goods too, and maybe if we freeze human beings there's a chance in a century they can be resurrected as 'real' human beings . . . Now, why do you try to save culture? As an anthropological reality it generates itself and it perishes by itself. It is a singularity, it has its birth and death, you don't need to attempt to save it. It has its own way. For me, it's useless to attempt to artificially perpetuate a system, because culture became a system of values. It's no longer an organic, symbolic organisation of sociality; now it's a system of market values, but of aesthetic values, not so much economic values. As a system of aesthetic values it is a very antinomic proposition, because culture perishes from this mixture of the symbolic and of values. The symbolic order of culture is not value; value is an economic structure. With infiltration or contamination of signs by an aesthetic circulation, and the rise of cultural goods as aesthetic goods, that's the beginning of the end.

WS *Exactly because you stockpile it, it's not culture. Culture should die. That's its honour. It's an anthropological event and should not be preserved for eternity, even if it sometimes happens.*

I'm only pessimistic, but you are a murderer. [*laughter and applause*]

Audience *Isn't difference the key to culture?*

No, we are in a culture of difference, of culture as difference, a multicultural organisation. Culture as singularity is more than difference. Difference can be easily organised into a system which generates structure and meaning. Culture as such has no finality, no meaning. It's a symbolic act, and in this sense it's beyond differences which are only oppositional structures. Singularity is a symbolic acting, a collective acting. Primitive societies and cultures are not different, they're very singular – it's not the same. Today, all cultures of the world are in multicultural ensembles as differences, together as the megaculture of difference, which is very opposed to the original singularity of culture.

WS *They are more like different brands.*

They can be juxtaposed and collected all together in a museum.

Audience *Do you think it's time that artists used their strengths for something else than making objects? Is there something an artist can do better than just contributing to the art market?*

An extension of art action today, in a very general sense, is performance. Maybe art is everywhere at this point, and as such it's possible to make art of everything. I'm afraid that's a pure extension of the ready-made. As a game, traditional art has a rule: it has to invent a scene other than reality. It must not work so much in the real world, to transform it in political, social, therapeutic ways. That's not art – art has a stronger, more radical definition for me. Today, it's a fact, art is an interacting, multidirectional activity, but that's a very degenerated art.

WS *What do you mean by radical?*

Radical would be the separation apart from any meaning, any finality, any causality. Art would be a thing itself, nothing but a singularity, and as such it cannot be anything in the real world. The art world would be anything else, it should be incompatible with reality. Traditional art was integrated in the symbolic order of the culture, but it was a radical illusion. In old times there wasn't reality. Now this illusion is lost, and art has lost its privileged position inside this symbolic order. Now we have to do with reality, and unfortunately contemporary art has fallen into the trap of reality, it becomes real, and soon it will be hyperreal in accordance with our surroundings. I would say rather than evolution it is an involution.

FU *I agree with your notion of the singularity of culture. I'm wondering though if you are – I don't think you are – talking about a closed system here, because in order to have singularity you need to have, just for the sake of comparison, a relation to otherness. That otherness is not to be confused with globalism or globalisation, but we need some way to be able to differentiate yourself from another in order to be single.*

I agree that the singularity has paradoxically to do with alterity. It's a paradigm which is highly opposed to 'identity/difference', which is our paradigm, I would say. Singularity and alterity is a double game, I agree.

FU *But that's not to be confused with what you have defined as globalisation, or multiculturalism.*

Yes, because we can oppose this paradigm of the totality of globalisation, where all differences can be integrated, but as differences, not as singularities. One of the strategies of this new order of the world is to transform singularities into differences. As differences they are able to be integrated into the global. As singularities they cannot. It's an immense attempt of this global world to reduce and annihilate all singularities in order to be integrated into an undifferentiated world. This world of differences, this culture of differences is an alibi for a culture of indifferentiation.

Audience *Regarding the stockpiling of culture, where is the room for the artist to have resistance? Do we go underground, like rats? True culture, like evil, cannot truly be suppressed.*

Of course, you may, or can, or must, but you must create your underground, because now there is no more underground, no more avant-garde, no more marginality. You can create your personal underground, your own black hole, your own singularity. The bad fate is that everyone can do that, but it will never create a collective symbolic order. It will be an exceptional, special creation, and today we can see that. Creative initiative, maybe as a subjective act, is very original but it doesn't create a symbolic movement. That's the problem.

WS *How do you see subjectivity coming to being? Is it still possible to have an authentic form of subjectivity?*

Why not? But today it would be a perversion. We are in a virtually positive, immanent world, where all is implicated in functional operations and so on. This arrangement doesn't need a subject any more. On the contrary, it must destroy subjectivity, and we can see that in this shifting from the subject to the individual. Today we speak always of the individual, the rights of the individual and so on. The individual is not the subject, the subject is over. The individual has no originality – it is a particular molecular fragment of an ensemble, and when you are in this system you are not a subject any more, you can be individual as an abstract configuration, but you are a pure operation, deducted from the functioning of a system. You are a by-product of the system as individual, instead of a subject with thoughts that generate actions. As a subject you were divided and alienated, of course. A subject is alienated, it is another subject. It effaces the other subjects. The individual has no other; everyone is individual. The other individual is not an other, it has no otherness, no alterity. We try to save subjectivity through intersubjectivity, interaction, but I don't believe in this escape.

WS *You would agree that in the future there could be another Baudrillard, as a by-product.*

As a clone. I am already a simulacrum of myself. You are not dealing with the real Baudrillard, I have sent a clone.

Audience *You said that the crisis is going to be intensified by globalisation, but you are not pessimistic. What are the reasons for not being pessimistic?*

It's not because I described or analysed a state of things this way: the order of things is nihilistic, it's the place for the exchange of nothing. I describe it but I take a distance from it. The form in the discourse, it's not only an analytic discourse; the theoretical discourse is also a form which is never pessimistic or optimistic, it's just a form. The salvation is in the form, not the content, even when you say the most pessimistic things. The content may be pessimistic or nihilistic, but the form, if it succeeds, is never either one, it is a transfiguration of the content. You do that in the writing. It's always a challenge between content and form, and that's the difference between a rational, discursive discourse and a theoretical approach. I, for my part, say the most nihilistic things, yes, but the resolution of this pessimistic content is in a very glorious form. Then the writing is not an innocent act, it is a transmutation of the content. That's why language is something very singular. It is always more than what it signifies, and you must take into account this transfiguration of language. It's always a challenge – you can describe the most apocalyptic system, but you can do it in a way that is not at all apocalyptic. The form can retain the singularity at the same time that it says something which is not singular but describes a non-singularity. It's always a duel.

WS *This kind of answers two questions I have here, concerning 'What happens in a simulated world where we have freedom from radical uncertainty – is there still a need for questions? After the orgy do we still need to ask questions? What kind of questions would these be?' You say that the content is not important, but the form can help you. You use the form of questioning.*

You take the example of the orgy, 'What are you doing after the orgy?' That is a question. There is no answer. The seduction, the paradox, the challenge is in the question itself. But we presuppose that the orgy is over, that we are at the end, or beyond the orgy: the orgy as a model of total liberation and integration. After that, there is no more a question of freedom, liberation, and so on. That's all been achieved, we are all liberated, liberated of needs, of language, of sex, but what is new after that? Maybe no answer is needed to this question. The orgy was an acting-out of all finalities, it was a model of the liberation of all things, it is a vanishing point. As a vanishing point it is very interesting, because after that we don't know what we are. But it's not very dangerous – to not know what we will and what we want and so on were the categories of Enlightenment and modern man. We are beyond that, and maybe it's a chance. We are free from freedom, free from liberation, that's over. Maybe now there's another chance, not for a new servitude . . . but maybe, maybe unknown models of servitude. We cannot have a radical moral judgement about these alternatives.

WS *So it's not that we are, as one question has here, 'just changing one set of truths for another'?*

We are changing our system of values, changing all our identities, our partners, our illusions, and so on. We are obliged to change, but changing is something other than becoming. They are different things. We are in a 'changing' time, where it is the moral law of all individuals, but changing is not becoming. We can change everything, we can change ourselves, but in this time we don't become anything. It was an opposition put forth by Nietzsche. He spoke about the era of chameleons. We are in a chameleonesque era, able to change but not able to become. This is our challenge. By an excess of potential changing, any possibility is there, but becoming is not a choice, becoming someone is another fatal strategy. For Nietzsche it would be the sovereign hypothesis. He speaks of four hypotheses. The first one would be inertia, motionlessness and so on. The second would be changing, the third one would be history, and the last one is the sovereign one, it is becoming. We are far away from becoming as a symbolic metamorphosis, as the symbolic return of things.

FU *The sovereignty consists in being free of some teleological perspective, becoming a sovereign consists in coming into being and passing away.*

In a sense, radical changing is also free from any finality, but it's simply a metastasis, it's not a metamorphosis, not becoming. Sovereignty has no finality, and changing doesn't either. Between the two we have a world with finality, meaning and so on. On either side we have changing and becoming – both have no finality but are radical opposites.

WS *Some specific questions. Does film possess the possibility to become an event, an* Ereignis, *as a pure image can become an event?*

I cannot say. I don't have enough experience with cinema. I enjoy it purely as a spectator, and I maintain this position as a stranger, which I would not sacrifice. Of course, nothing is excluded from singularity. It's a question of complexity – with the pure image in photography, we can have a determined frame for analysis, from what we subtracted: the noise, the meaning, the motion. If we go to the moving image, I don't know what happens exactly. For me it's too complex to be analysed as pure. Of course a pure image is a fantasy. Cinema has prestige as a progress from photography – in our rational consideration, there is a progress which is supposed to lead to a sophistication, a perfection. I think the contrary: every progress in this area is at the same time a danger. It's always a risk of degeneration. That is not nostalgic, I don't consider the pure image as a lost object. We must judge any complexification as at the same time a plus and a minus.

WS *Would that also apply to another question: 'Do you see the Internet as a manifestation of singularity?' You say on the one hand it's not complexity as such, you have to judge by looking closely at what happens on the Internet. Are there not singularities, people setting up their own space . . . ?*

At this point I'm sure there is no singularity on the Internet. That's not because I don't use the Internet. I'm technically, physically not able to use it, but that's not a doctrine, my refusal is not ideological. What constitutes singularity is exactly not this immanence, this overall possibility of play with identity, with communication. This is precisely the contrary of a singularity. It's rather an artistic activity. That's not a pejorative. In this virtual secluded world, there is no alterity at all, no dual relation. There is inter-individual interaction, there is interaction with oneself, but no alterity, no challenge in this sense. But it can be a place for infinite complexity, yes.

WS *You are the best example. I think there are 800 websites concerning you, and all of them are very different. They all say 'My Baudrillard' . . .*

It's not a compliment, I am a hostage on the Internet.

WS *We have many questions on the topic of seduction. 'In your model of seduction, why is vengeance necessary when the pact is broken?'*

First, I don't have a model of seduction. It's a form, a dual relation, not a model. Of course it's a pact, not a contract. When you break the pact, one form of challenge and reversibility is revenge. Revenge is a vital acting-out. It preserves the status of the other, maybe in a violent form, in a murder for example. A murder can be a very dualistic act, a pact which allows us to see that there is a deeper complicity in revenge than in indifference. Indifference is a very despisal of the other. That's our reaction, today. The most frequent reaction to all negative happening is an indifferent response, not revenge.

WS *Finally, here is an interesting hypothetical situation: 'What if the United States, in an enormous celebration, destroyed the Statue of Liberty itself, before terrorists had the chance? Would this be a sufficient counter-gift to September 11, by reclaiming the "privilege of death"?'*

That's a good idea . . .

WS *'If so, what ground, if any, would terrorism have left, once the destruction of the exceptional has lost its power as a singular event?'*

I would very much like to see the Statue of Liberty destroyed. It would not be an event because it would not be the first event, it would be a clone event of the Twin Towers . . . too bad, too bad. It would not be the end of terrorism just because there would be nothing more to destroy with planes – terrorism has multiple forms of appearances. We are now fantastically obsessed with this figure of the Twin Towers, it's impermissible to imagine other forms of terrorism which would be not so spectacular. It's a very exceptional event, a very exceptional acting-out, but maybe it's still spectacular, in the sense that it's a global event and a symptom of globalisation. Maybe there are more viral, more underground forms of terrorism than this one. This one opened an era of a new type of violence, a violence of the third type. There will be more subtle modes of terrorism, and I doubt if Pentagon strategists have any idea of that.

NOTE

1. See V. Grace, H. Worth and L. Simmons (eds) (2003), *Baudrillard West of the Dateline*, Palmerston, New Zealand: Dunmore Press, pp. 23–36. [Editors]

18 The Catastrophe of Paradox

In December 1992, Baudrillard was in the United Kingdom and delivered the lecture 'Hyperreal America'.[1] This is a transcription of the questions and answers that the talk provoked.

Audience *You referred to Biosphere II[2] as being hyperreal. I would like to know why Biosphere II is any more hyperreal or any less real than America? And also, what is the real America?*

Yes, what is the real America? I cannot say that. Who knows? [*laughter*] But what I would say is that between the real America and the hyperreal America there is virtually no possible distinction, and that an example of that is the potential confusion between Biosphere II and the everyday life of America around it. The principle of simulation lies not in the idea that the real is false, but that the very distinction between false and true is impossible, that is simulation. It seems to me that life in America can be considered as a film, a movie, and you cannot distinguish between a movie and America. You cannot experience things beyond this hyperreality of films, signs and so on and get to its core, its reality. It is impossible, but it would be a very bad experience if there was still a nostalgia for reality. We as Europeans experience very nostalgically and very unfortunately the distortion between reality and imaginary. For us Europeans, the distortion is a very unfortunate one, but for Americans, or when we are in America, the distinction vanishes, and then it is no more the imaginary of a real but of a lost object. It functions, but we must take cognisance, and then it is a hyperreality. There is no more real, no more imaginary, but hyperreality – another experience, a very original one I would say.

Audience *Do you not think this hyperreality is spreading back to Europe with, for example, the nation's youth playing video games?*

[Further clarification:] In Europe, we are not getting the same hyperreality. We are perhaps just a couple of generations behind?

I do not believe that. Of course we are invaded by all this hypermodern, hyperreal means of communication and so on, and everyday life, thanks to thought by analogy, by exports, tends to become the same way as the American way of life. But I have to speak as French. I do not know if it is the same for the English. I have the impression that we will never become modern. Maybe we have hypermodern, hyperreal features; we assume that. But we have not become really modern. This new hyperspace, we do not experience it because we have no space for that. And we must assume our historical past, and we must manage with that, and the whole thing is very complicated. America has no history; they do not need to metabolise time, history (relatively of course). They do not need that, because it started from a zero point. We will never conquer this point – it is impossible; it is too late. The originality, that expanse has become monstrous and at the same time very wonderful, is an outcome that will never become part of our history. I prefer to assume things as different, as radically different, as antagonistic rather than as evolutionistic, virtually the same. We become Americans? No, I do not think that. But that is not a compliment. I prefer to experience this new world as an exoticism, as very exotic. I do not think things will converge in a mondial.

Audience *You portray America as a country in which it is impossible to perceive reality behind the ways in which the country represents itself to itself by way of all sorts of imagery. Now I wonder if that is not what you would say in looking at the middle classes in America? What I find missing from your account is what it must look like for those who can see pretty clearly that a lot of what America promises is false in their lives, who coming up against what is not provided by just the sorts of imagery that you portray, and which certainly does deliver for a certain class of people. But that is a lot of America that is missing in your account.*

Yes, I do not contend that. I take no account of all the political aspects of America, and so on. I cannot do that. I do not say anyway that America is an ideal country where all classes are very happy, even in the imaginary. My point of view is European. I said that at the beginning. It is a fiction. I try to look at America through the spectrum of what America invented as the imaginary, as a self-fiction. And maybe the Americans themselves are very deceived by this distortion between fiction and real life, which is very great. But I consider that from another point of view, and I would say, very passionately, something like a prejudice, but I assume this prejudice, I cannot do it in any other way. I am not American. I cannot experience this country from the inside; I am outside of that. My only defence is that I take the challenge of being contested by the reality because reality will never assume the other of hyperreality. But I cannot live as a real American. As a European, I am a fictional American. Maybe the reverse is equally true, as a real American can never experience Europe as another way. I cannot, and I will not, excuse this challenge. It may be contested in all ways, especially if you speak politically or economically and so on. However, I would say that even the real contradictions in the American way of life, the political ones and so on, are not exactly 'real'; they are never real, they are always mediated through a fictional way. They are always overlegitimised in another utopia – what I call an 'achieved utopia', a sort of catastrophe of paradox because realisation and utopia are contrary. This creates a sort of basis common to all Americans that changes in some way their own perception of their own lives.

Audience *Just a small point of clarification. I heard you say that the world has no centre. I was wondering whether you mean that it no longer has any one centre or that there are no centres? [Further clarification:] Are there no centres whatsoever, completely without any kind of coordination, where everything must be floating, or is there no longer one hegemonic centre? I am not so sure what that means if you say there is no centre. Then you are actually saying that there are no other positions or no other possibilities for people to hang onto and everything just becomes a kind of flux of electromagnetic messages going around about without a way of condensing them around something. No resistance, no other cultures, no other traditions that can resist that. Or are you saying that now we are in a position that, what used to be, say since the last forty or fifty years, the centre is no longer that quite a powerful a centre any more?*

By definition, if there is no centre any more, there are no centres. I mean the world has become eccentric. There are not several centres; it is eccentric. And these polarities function otherwise than a centre. There are singularities, different models; they do not converge in a centrality, a mondiality, a totality of the world. There are singularities but they function antagonistically, against one another. And this is no more a potentially unified world than it was in the universal system of values of the Western culture. It is something else, we can no longer think of a centre. Before it was a kind of *Weltanschauung,* a mondial point of view where everything converged through gravity towards the centre. And maybe this gravitation has had to reverse itself. And now things do not converge any more to a centre. On the contrary, it would be a dissemination into the void. Not only is this not only one centre, but the concept of gravitation itself has reversed – it is the antigravitation of this new world. There cannot be any centre any more. The very problem is that even gravitation has disappeared, and in its place there is a very different virtuality, of escaping, of disseminating in the void of space. Also, I would say America is interesting in this sense too, that it is an America in anticipation of this state of things. It was a centre, but this centre was never the centre. From the beginning, it was always potentially dissemination of the centre, potentially antigravitation. That I found fascinating.

Audience *Are you saying that the experience of the hyperreal cuts across all class, ethnic and racial lines? Or are you saying that it is just your experience of the United States as a European? I am not quite clear on that, I must confess.*

If it were my own exclusive experience, I would not speak. [Why?] It is useless. I think that it has a reality, not verification though. It makes sense or I would not speak, but I would say that this experience, just because it is mine, I can extrapolate it, a fiction maybe, to all people. I would not call it a political or economic analysis. I cannot do that. As hypothetical, it is valuable for all people, all classes, all places, and all parts of the Third World, and so on. But just because it is my experience and singular, its singularity, its specificity allows me to extend this in an extrapolation. Because I do not insist on reality, I do not contend that my representation is true, and if it is not true, I can extend it to all reality. It will be fiction; it will never conform to verification or truth – that is the principle. I do not pretend to be subject to verification and so on. At the same time, it is very singular, very passionate, specific, and potentially extrapolatable to all reality or hyperreality. Beyond that, I would say if we relate it as transpolitically, I would say that the very reality (it is very contradictory to say that, but) the very stubborn reality of the cultural world is not the reality of the classical world, of classes and historical contradiction, of the Third World and so on. Not this, but the irruption of the Fourth World, a sort of unidentifiable other world, other transpolitical world, not political in the traditional sense. Not geographical, it is no longer geographical, but it is in the core of the system itself. It is in the very logic of the system itself. That is real, actual. And this new world, not exactly underground, rather viral, fractal, eccentric and so on – a new reality that coincides with my hyperreality.

Audience *I would like to come back to something you said about the real past and nostalgia. There has to be an experience in order to be nostalgic about it?*

Yes. You said we must have experienced something to be nostalgic about it. Yes, I get the point. The American world is not nostalgic. We are nostalgic because we have a history, we have an origin and we have finalities. We must be nostalgic now because these values, these finalities, are disappearing more or less. The American world is not nostalgic in this sense. Americans are not nostalgic. I can get out of this complex nostalgic feedback of our culture – the possible revival of history that we experience here in Europe. I would say not nostalgia in this sense, but maybe another nuance, another meaning of melancholy, not the absence of another system, not nostalgia because of a lost object, but the melancholy of things would be connected with the dissemination of things, with its immediacy, singularity, the instantaneity of materialisation. Maybe behind that it is a sort of illusion, optical illusion, an illusion of perception, a self-deception. This may always happen, all is possible, that generates a world with a certain melancholy, but not nostalgia.

Audience (continued) *Sorry, I cannot help being critical of this concept of nostalgia because for one, we have to be critical of nostalgia about really old values, why these are specific to certain social groups like women.*

I mean in a world where utopia and nostalgia are connected, one in the past and the other in the future, utopia and nostalgia are properties, tonalities of our culture. When the achievement is not in the future, it is here; there is no nostalgia any more. Maybe there is violence; there are unbearable events, but another thing. You must take account of the instantaneity of things. You cannot change things through a return, a feedback, or history to past events. It must be managed in a topical, strategic instantaneity. Maybe it changes the concept of practice of events. Maybe not; I do not know. But it will be a general condition that any, even political, will, or movement must take account of this ephemerality, pure actuality, or instantaneity of things. And through very concrete things, media, mass media. Instantaneity of values, values of this or that group lose their sense. Things have sense when they have an origin and a future, a beginning and a finality. There is direction and sense. But when time is short-circuited, imploded in an instant, there is no sense, or at least not the same sense.

Audience *Are you saying that the United States was always hyperreal? Or, if you are not saying that, when did it become hyperreal?*

That is a trap! [*laughter*] I would like to say that it was always hyperreal from the very beginning, because the rupture with Europe was a very special condition. People who are displaced, that are deterritorialised in this way, geographically and *malgré tout* are in a very specific state, and from the beginning it is something very special, which will never be replaced. It may be the fundamental feature of this hyperreality – that is why we will never experience this, because we will never have been displaced in this sense. Of course, we could not say that hyperreality was here before all the modernity, of all the modern world, the technical transformation and take-off of America in this direction. It would be very uncertain to speak of hyperreality in this sense. But once more, I cannot choose between the two. I would like to keep the principle that hyperreality was there from the beginning, but the realisation of hyperreality is a process that needs a sort of modernity; it is historical.

Audience *Jean Baudrillard spoke of the American city, but he did not address the question of small American suburbs, White suburbs that seem to be founded upon an exclusion of non-White persons. How does that fit in the experience of the American city?*

I spoke, of course, about these cities generally as a modern city, and not sociologically and so on. I am sorry I cannot do that, and others can do that better than me. The problem is always the same, to point to the fact that these American cities from the beginning have no centre, no monuments, no history; the dimension is vertical and rather exponential. This concerns all people in the cities, just by the very fact that there is no centre of grandeur at the heart of this eccentric city. These problems of the ghettos, suburbs, downtown centres are part of an eccentric ensemble. These metropolises, that have no centre, become the centre of the world, as with New York. This is a paradox of these cities, and the problems of ghettos and so on. I cannot explain. In contradiction with European and French cities, where discrimination is very superior/inferior with a particular content, the high culture to the low or the non-culture of the immigrants, and so on. I would say that in the American cities all races perhaps have a chance of a future antagonism that does exist in Europe. And the various American cities have this antagonism, this multiplicity of race and so on, and that is no reason to advocate multiculturalism and so on. It is already, was built in this way. It is another process in Europe.

Audience *Doesn't your very definition of America as brief history of the origin of hyperreality by definition exclude the indigenous peoples of America? And when you say that we in Europe must have to pursue our history, we cannot avoid it, but America is not like that, there is no comparison. Isn't your position then complicit with a certain will in America to avoid responsibility for aspects of its history and current political effects of that? [Further clarification:] That this particular account of America as modernity, as something that Europe will never be, as completely unlike us, to say that seems to me to be complicit with a refusal in the United States to accept certain aspects of its history, and that goes along with certain refusals in the law courts?*

There is a misunderstanding. I do not refuse these problems, these problems of indigenous peoples. I am conscious that the American world is built on the original murder of the indigenous people. I would not contest that. You cannot make justice with an absence of origin. The indigenous people that have been murdered will never be rehabilitated even if they get their rights, their human rights and so on. The murder is not an origin as in Europe, a continuity, a dialectic of culture and so on. It is a murder, a rupture; this symbolic rupture with the territory, with human beings that were in this territory, is analogous to this rupture with the very origins in Europe. There is a double rupture, a double paradox I would say. But I cannot assume the human part of that pathetic situation. I do not refuse that, but I cannot take an account in such an analysis. I do not refuse this . . .

Audience *You say that you cannot, but your discourse is actually complicit with that . . .*

No. If you say that, we are on another logic.

Chairperson *Do you want to expand on that question?*

Audience *No. I don't actually. I don't want to be sucked into this . . .*

You can say I am a racist, a fascist, and so on but . . .

Audience *The same question that everyone else seems to be asking. Which is, can you be a cultural observer without being a social theorist? That is the general thing. I am not American, and I have never been to America, but I heard something on Radio 4 [laughter] which really shocked me, and that is that more and more wealthy Americans are choosing to incarcerate themselves in secure complexes which are policed, have modern conveniences, and are cut off from society. They are essentially White middle-class prisons that are defined against a second state of nature. That seems to me to be bizarre, and has some similarities with the hyperreality you ascribed to Disneyland. Only there in these prison complexes, there is an inside and there is an outside, and the people who are on the inside have objective reasons why they want to stay there.*

Chairperson *That is not true of Disneyland? [Further clarification]*

Audience *There is a difference there with Disneyland. I would like to hear what you could say about the hyperreality of these prison complexes.*

This example, this closure as a jail, as a secure way of life, it is the same comparison between Biosphere II and the real everyday way of life; I mean in this system I described, this as a catastrophe, not as an ideal world. Biosphere II is an embodiment of this. I mean each of us lives potentially in a cell, in a jail. Today, it may be an electronic one, a computerised one, a media one, or something like that. But we are all in this bubble, just as the child that was enclosed in the bubble, with wires and tubes and so on.[3] He has no real life; he is very secure and very protected, but he cannot go back into real life, he will be dead. We are all in this case; I mean, this is a special example, a visible example, a very common condition of people in this new world. We are all potential clones in our own bubble, and we may prefer this synthetic security to another world with its conflicts. But hyperreality, it is a way to escape reality – all the conflicts, risks, the seduction – it escapes from sexuality, alterity and so forth. This example is very significant.

Transcribed by Richard G. Smith

NOTES

1. See J. Baudrillard (1993), 'Hyperreal America', *Economy & Society* 22(2), 243–52.
2. See J. Baudrillard (1992), 'La Biosphère II', in A.-M. Eyssartel and B. Rochette (eds), *Des Mondes Inventés – Les Parcs à Thème*, Paris: Editions de la Villette, pp. 126–30.
3. See J. Baudrillard (1985), 'The Child in the Bubble', *Impulse* 11(4), 12–13.

19 This is the Fourth World War

Interview with Romain Leick (RL)

RL *Monsieur Baudrillard, you have described the 9/11 attacks on New York and Washington as the 'absolute event'. You have accused the United States, with its insufferable hegemonic superiority, of rousing the desire for its own destruction. Now that the reign of the Taliban has collapsed pitifully and Bin Laden is nothing more than a hunted fugitive, don't you have to retract everything?*

I have glorified nothing, accused nobody, justified nothing. One should not confuse the messenger with his message. I have endeavoured to analyse the process through which the unbounded expansion of globalisation creates the conditions for its own destruction.

RL *In the process, don't you simply deflect attention from the fact that there are identifiable criminals and terrorists who are responsible for the attacks?*

Of course there are those who committed these acts, but the spirit of terrorism and panic reaches far beyond them. The Americans' war is focused on a visible object, which they would like to destroy. Yet the event of September 11th, in all of its symbolism, cannot be obliterated in this manner. The bombing of Afghanistan is a completely inadequate, substitute action.

RL *All the same, the United States has brought to an end a barbaric form of oppression and, in the process, has given the Afghani people an opportunity for a new, peaceful beginning. Or at least this is how your colleague, Bernard-Henri Lévy, sees it.*

The situation doesn't appear to me as so unequivocal. Lévy's triumphalism strikes me as strange. He treats B-52 bombers as if they were instruments of the world-spirit.

RL *So there is no such thing as a just war?*

No, there's always too much ambivalence. Wars are often begun in the name of justice, indeed this is almost always the official justification. Yet, while they themselves want to be so justified and are undertaken with the best of intentions, they normally don't end in the manner in which their instigators had imagined.

RL *The Americans have attained some unquestionable successes. Many Afghans are now able to hope for a better life.*

You wait and see. Not all the Afghani women have discarded their veils yet. Sharia is still in effect. Without a doubt, the Taliban regime has been smashed. However, the network of the international terror organisation, al-Qaida, still exists. And Bin Laden, dead or alive, has, above all, disappeared. This lends him a mythical power; he has achieved a certain supernatural quality.

RL *The Americans would be successful only if they were able to present Bin Laden or his body on television?*

That would be a questionable spectacle, and he himself would continue to play the role of martyr. Such an exhibition would not necessarily demystify him. What is at issue is more than the control of a territory or a population, or the disbanding of a subversive organisation. The stakes have become metaphysical.

RL *Why can't you simply accept that the destruction of the World Trade Center was an arbitrary, irrational act of blind fanatics?*

A good question, but, even if it were a matter of addressing the catastrophe in-itself, it would still have symbolic meaning. Its fascination can only be explained in this way. Here something happened that far exceeded the will of the actors. There is a general allergy to an ultimate order, to an ultimate power, and the Twin Towers of the World Trade Center embodied this in the fullest sense.

RL *Thus, you explain terroristic delusion as the unavoidable reaction against a system which has itself become megalomaniacal?*

With its totalising claim, the system created the conditions for this horrible retaliation. The immanent mania of globalisation generates madness, just as an unstable society produces delinquents and psychopaths. In truth, these are only symptoms of the sickness. Terrorism is everywhere, like a virus. It doesn't require Afghanistan as its home base.

RL *You suggest that globalisation and resistance to it is like the course of an illness, even to the point of self-destruction. Is this not what is particularly scandalous about your analysis – that it completely leaves out morality?*

In my own way, I am very much a moralist. There is a morality of analysis, a duty of honesty. That is to say, it is immoral to close one's eyes to the truth, to find excuses, in order to cover up that which is difficult to bear. We must see the thing beyond the opposition of good and bad. I seek a confrontation with the event as it is without equivocation. Anyone who is unable to do that is led to a moral falsification of history.

RL *But if the terrorist act takes place as a form of compulsion or fate, as you claim, is it not then at the same time exculpated? There is no longer a morally responsible subject.*

It is clear to me that the conceptual nature of my analysis is doubled-edged. Words can be turned against me. However, I do not praise murderous attacks – that would be idiotic. Terrorism is not a contemporary form of revolution against oppression and capitalism. No ideology, no struggle for an objective, not even Islamic fundamentalism, can explain it.

RL *But why should globalisation turn against itself? Why should it run amok, when, after all, it promises freedom, well-being and happiness for all?*

That is the utopian view, the advertisement, more or less. Yet there is altogether no positive system. In general, all the positive historical utopias are extremely murderous, as fascism and communism have shown.

RL *Surely you cannot compare globalisation with the bloodiest systems of the twentieth century?*

It is based, as colonialism was earlier, on immense violence. It creates more victims than beneficiaries, even when the majority of the Western world profits from it. Naturally the United States, in principle, could liberate every country just as it has liberated Afghanistan. But what kind of peculiar liberation would that be? Those so fortunate would know how to defend themselves even with terror if necessary.

RL *Do you hold globalisation to be a form of colonialism, disguised as the widening of Western civilisation?*

It is pitched as the endpoint of the Enlightenment, the solution to all contradictions. In reality, it transforms everything into a negotiable, quantifiable exchange value. This process is extremely violent, for it cashes up in the idea of unity as the ideal state, in which everything that is unique, every singularity, including other cultures and finally every non-monetary value would be incorporated. See, on this point, I am the humanist and moralist.

RL *But don't universal values such as freedom, democracy and human rights also establish themselves through globalisation?*

One must differentiate radically between the global and the universal. The universal values, as the Enlightenment defined them, constitute a transcendental ideal. They confront the subject with its own freedom, which is a permanent task and responsibility, not simply a right. This is completely absent in the global, which is an operational system of total trade and exchange.

RL *Rather than liberating humanity, globalisation only in turn reifies it?*

It pretends to liberate people, only to deregulate them. The elimination of all rules, more precisely the reduction of all rules to laws of the market, is the opposite of freedom – namely, its illusion. Such outdated and aristocratic values as dignity, honesty, challenge and sacrifice no longer count for anything.

RL *Doesn't the unrestricted recognition of human rights build a decisive bulwark against this alienating process?*

I think that human rights have already been integrated into the process of globalisation and therefore function as an alibi. They belong to a juridical and moral superstructure; in short, they are advertising.

RL *Therefore mystification?*

Isn't it a paradox that the West uses the following motto as a weapon against dissenters: 'Either you share our values or . . .'? A democracy asserted with threats and blackmail only sabotages itself. It no longer represents the autonomous decision for freedom, but rather becomes a global imperative. This is, in effect, a perversion of Kant's categorical imperative, which implies freely chosen consent to its command.

RL *So the end of history, the absolute sway of democracy, would be a new form of world dictatorship?*

Yes, and it is completely inconceivable that there would be no violent counter-reaction against it. Terrorism emerges when no other form of resistance seems possible. The system takes as objectively terrorist whatever is set against it. The values of the West are ambivalent. At one point in time they could have a positive effect and accelerate progress, at another, however, they drive themselves to such extremes that they falsify themselves and ultimately turn against their own purpose.

RL *If the antagonism between globalisation and terrorism in reality is irresolvable, then what purpose could the War against Terrorism still have?*

US President Bush aspires to return to trusted ground by rediscovering the balance between friend and foe. The Americans are prosecuting this war as if they were defending themselves against a wolf pack. But this doesn't work against viruses that have already been in us for a long time. There is no longer a front, no demarcation line; the enemy sits in the heart of the culture that fights it. That is, if you like, the Fourth World War: no longer between peoples, states, systems and ideologies, but, rather, of the human species against itself.

RL *Then in your opinion this war cannot be won?*

No one can say how it will all turn out. What hangs in the balance is the survival of humanity, it is not about the victory of one side. Terrorism has no political project, it has no finality; though it is seen as real, it is absurd.

RL *Bin Laden and the Islamists do indeed have a social project, an image of a rigorous, ideal community in the name of Allah.*

Perhaps, but it is not religiosity that drives them to terrorism. All the Islam experts emphasise this. The assassins of September 11th made no demands. Fundamentalism is a symptomatic form of rejection, refusal; its adherents didn't want to accomplish anything concrete, they simply rise up wildly against what they perceive as a threat to their own identity.

RL *Yet this doesn't change the fact that in the course of history cultural evolution takes place. Doesn't the global expansion of Western culture demonstrate the power of its appeal?*

Why not also say its superiority? Cultures are like languages. Each is incommensurable, a self-contained work of art for itself. There is no hierarchy of languages. One cannot measure them against universal standards. It is theoretically possible for a language to assert itself globally. However, such reduction would constitute an absolute danger.

RL *For all intents and purposes, you refuse the idea of moral progress. The unique, which you defend, is in itself not a value at all. It can be good or evil, selfless or criminal . . .*

Yes, singularity can assume all forms, including the vicious or terroristic. It remains, all the same, an artwork. For the rest, I don't believe that there are predominantly good or evil cultures – there are, of course, disastrous diversions, but it is not possible to separate the one from the other. Evil does not retreat in proportion to the advance of the good. Therefore the concept of progress is, outside of the rationality of the natural sciences, in fact, problematic. Montaigne said: 'If the evil in men were eliminated, then the fundamental condition of life would be destroyed.'

RL *No heaven without hell, no redemption without perdition – isn't your dualistic view of the world nothing more than pessimism and fatalism?*

Fatalism offers an unpalatable interpretation of the world, for it leads to resignation. I don't resign myself. I want clarity, a lucid consciousness.

When we know the rules of the game, then we can change them. In this respect, I am a man of the Enlightenment.

RL *But your knowledge of evil doesn't lead you to combat it.*

No, for me that is senseless. Good and evil are irresolvably bound up with one another. This is fatal in the original sense: an integral part of our fate, our destiny.

RL *Why does Western culture find it so difficult to tolerate the existence of evil? Why is it repressed and denied?*

Evil was interpreted as misfortune, for misfortune can be combated: poverty, injustice, oppression and so on. This is the humanitarian view of things, the pathetic and sentimental vision, the permanent empathy with the wretched. Evil is the world as it is and as it has been. Misfortune is the world as it never should have been. The transformation of evil into misfortune is the most lucrative industry of the twentieth century.

RL *While evil cannot be exorcised, misfortune can be made good, it demands a better condition.*

Misfortune is a mine whose ore is inexhaustible. Evil, in contrast, can't be subdued by any form of rationality. This is the illusion of the West: because technological perfection seems within reach, one believes by extension in the possibility of realising moral perfection, in a future free of contingencies in the best of all possible worlds. Everything should be redeemed – which is what comprises the contemporary ideal of our democracy. Everything will be genetically manipulated in order to attain the biological and democratic perfection of the human species.

RL *Do you regret that the West has lost its belief in redemption through God?*

You know, in reality one would have to turn the whole debate on its head. The exciting question is not why there is evil. First there is evil, without question. Why is there good? This is the real miracle.

RL *Could you explain it without reference to God?*

In the eighteenth century, Rousseau and others tried, but not very convincingly. The best and simplest hypothesis is, in effect, to postulate God. God is like democracy: the least corrupt and therefore the best of all possible solutions.

RL *When one hears you, it is possible to conclude that you would have been a Cathar in the Middle Ages.*

Oh yes, I love the world of the Cathars because I am Manichaean.

RL *[You are] of the opinion that there is an eternal opposition between light and night, good and evil . . .*

. . . Yes, the Cathars held the material world to be evil and bad, created by demons. At the same time, they put their faith in God, the holy and the possibility of perfection. This is a much more radical view than that which sees in evil only the gradually diminishing auxiliaries of the good.

RL *Monsieur Baudrillard, thank you for this interview.*

Translated by Samir Gandesha

20 The Matrix Decoded

Interview with Aude Lancelin (AL)

AL *Your reflections on reality and the virtual are some of the key references used by the makers of* The Matrix. *The first episode explicitly referred to you as the viewer clearly saw the cover of* Simulacra and Simulation. *Were you surprised by this?*

Certainly there have been misinterpretations, which is why I have been hesitant until now to speak about *The Matrix*. The staff of the Wachowski brothers contacted me at various times following the release of the first episode in order to get me involved with the following ones, but this wasn't really conceivable [*laughter*]. Basically, a similar misunderstanding occurred in the 1980s when New York-based Simulationist artists contacted me. They took the hypothesis of the virtual for an irrefutable fact and transformed it into a visible phantasm. But it is precisely that we can no longer employ categories of the real in order to discuss the characteristics of the virtual.

AL *The connection between the film and the vision you develop, for example, in* The Perfect Crime, *is, however, quite striking. In evoking 'a desert of the real', these totally virtualised spectral humans, who are no more than the energetic reserve of thinking objects . . .*

Yes, but already there have been other films that treat the growing indistinction between the real and the virtual: *The Truman Show*, *Minority Report*, or even *Mulholland Drive*, the masterpiece of David Lynch. *The Matrix*'s value is chiefly as a synthesis of all that. But there the set-up is cruder and does not truly evoke the problem. The actors are in the matrix, that is, in the digitised system of things; or they are radically outside it, such as in Zion, the city of resistors. But what would be interesting would be to show what happens when these two worlds collide.

The most embarrassing part of the film is that the new problem posed by simulation is confused with its classical, Platonic treatment. This is a serious flaw. The radical illusion of the world is a problem faced by all great cultures, which they have solved through art and symbolisation. What we have invented, in order to support this suffering, is a simulated real, which henceforth supplants the real and is its final solution, a virtual universe from which everything dangerous and negative has been expelled. And *The Matrix* is undeniably part of that. Everything belonging to the order of dream, utopia and phantasm is given expression, 'realised'. We are in the uncut transparency. *The Matrix* is surely the kind of film about the matrix that the matrix would have been able to produce.

AL *It is also a film that purports to denounce technicist alienation, and at the same time plays entirely on the fascination exercised by the digital universe and computer-generated images.*

What is notable about *Matrix Reloaded* is the absence of any glimmer of irony that would allow viewers to turn this gigantic special effect on its head. There is no sequence which would be the *punctum* about which Roland Barthes wrote, this striking mark that brings you face-to-face with a true image. Moreover, this is what makes the film an instructive symptom, and the actual fetish of this universe of technologies of the screen in which there is no longer a distinction between the real and the imaginary. *The Matrix* is considered to be an extravagant object, at once candid and perverse, where there is neither a here nor a there. The pseudo-Freud who speaks at the film's conclusion puts it well: at a certain moment, we reprogrammed the matrix in order to integrate anomalies into the equation. And you, the resistors, comprise a part of it. Thus we are, it seems, within a total virtual circuit without an exterior. Here again I am in theoretical disagreement [*laughter*]. *The Matrix* paints the picture of a monopolistic superpower, like we see today, and then collaborates in its refraction. Basically, its dissemination on a world scale is complicit with the film itself. On this point it is worth recalling Marshall McLuhan: the medium is the message. The message of *The Matrix* is its own diffusion by an uncontrollable and proliferating contamination.

AL *It is rather shocking to see that, henceforth, all American marketing successes, from* The Matrix *to Madonna's new album, are presented as critiques of the system which massively promotes them.*

That is exactly what makes our times so oppressive. The system produces a negativity in *trompe l'oeil*, which is integrated into products of the spectacle just as obsolescence is built into industrial products. It is the most efficient way of incorporating all genuine alternatives. There are no longer external Omega points or any antagonistic means available to analyse the world; there is nothing more than a fascinated adhesion. One must understand, however, that the more a system nears perfection, the more it approaches the total accident. It is a form of objective irony stipulating that nothing ever happened. September 11th participated in this. Terrorism is not an alternative power; it is nothing except the metaphor of this almost suicidal return of Western power on itself. That is what I said at the time, and it was not widely accepted. But it is not about being nihilistic or pessimistic in the face of all that. The system, the virtual, the matrix – all of these will perhaps return to the dustbin of history. For reversibility, challenge and seduction are indestructible.

Translated by Gary Genosko and Adam Bryx

21 Continental Drift

Interview with Deborah Solomon (DS)

DS *As one of France's most celebrated philosophers, can you give us any insight into the civil discontent that is pitting a generation of young people against the rest of the country?*

It will get worse and worse and worse. For a long time, it was a relatively friendly coexistence or cohabitation, but the French haven't done much to integrate the Muslims, and there is a split now. Our organic sense of identity as a country has been split.

DS *Perhaps that was inevitable. Many of us here were surprised last year when the French government banned hijabs, head scarves, and other religious emblems from public schools.*

Yes, in America there is more of a history of immigration. America is constituted by ethnic communities, and though they may compete with one another, America is still America. Even if there were no Americans living in the United States, there would still be America. France is just a country; America is a concept.

DS *Are you saying that America represents the ideal of democracy?*

No, the simulation of power.

DS *At 76, you are still pushing your famous theory about 'simulation' and the 'simulacrum', which maintains that media images have become more convincing and real than reality.*

All of our values are simulated. What is freedom? We have a choice between buying one car or buying another car? It's a simulation of freedom.

DS *So you don't think that the US invaded Iraq to spread freedom?*

What we want is to put the rest of the world on the same level of masquerade and parody that we are on, to put the rest of the world into simulation, so all the world becomes total artifice and then we are all-powerful. It's a game.

DS *When you say 'we', who are you talking about? In your new book,* The Conspiracy of Art, *you are pretty hard on this country.*

France is a by-product of American culture. We are all in this; we are globalised. When Jacques Chirac says 'No!' to Bush about the Iraq war, it's a delusion. It's to insist on the French as an exception, but there is no French exception.

DS *Hardly. France chose not to send soldiers to Iraq, which has real meaning for countless individual soldiers, for their families and for the state.*

Ah, yes. We are 'against' the war because it is not our war. But in Algeria, it was the same. America didn't send soldiers when we fought the Algerian war. France and America are on the same side. There is only one side.

DS *Isn't that kind of simplistic reasoning why people get so tired of French intellectuals?*

There are no more French intellectuals. What you call French intellectuals have been destroyed by the media. They talk on television, they talk to the press, and they are no longer talking among themselves.

DS *Do you think there are intellectuals in America?*

For us, there was Susan Sontag and Noam Chomsky. But that is French chauvinism. We count ourselves. We don't pay attention to what comes from outside. We accept only what we invented.

DS *Were you a friend of Susan Sontag?*

We saw each other from time to time, but the last time it was terrible. She came to a conference in Toronto and blasted me for having denied that reality exists.

DS *Do you read the work of any American writers?*

I read many, many American novelists. Updike, Philip Roth, Truman Capote. I prefer American fiction to French fiction.

DS *Perhaps French literature fell prey to French theory?*

Unfortunately, French literature starved itself. It didn't need French theory in order to die. It died by itself.

DS *Some here feel that the study of the humanities at our universities has been damaged by the incursion of deconstruction and other French theories.*

That was the gift of the French. They gave Americans a language they did not need. It was like the Statue of Liberty. Nobody needs French theory.

22 The Art of Disappearing

Interview with Truls Lie (TL)

A MAGNIFICIENT GAME

TL *How are we to understand the relationship between the playful game and the dominant value-regimes' insistence on production and consumption? One could of course say that today's production satisfies a positive and playful desire to create. Even though there is overproduction of virtually everything, there may just be a 'playful human' behind the scenes. You convey it as problematic that people play an active role in today's overproduction, but why shouldn't this be based on play, on a productive desire, as Gilles Deleuze would have it?*

Think of it all as a magnificent game, where certain things come to represent more and more other things. Playing and games have several dimensions that have been categorised by the sociologist Roger Caillois: Mimicry (the game of representation), Alea (the game of chance), Agon (rivalry and competition), and last but not least, Ilinx, the vertiginous, delirious dimension inherent in some games. Our modern production, overproduction, and overabundance of communication and information correspond to a vertiginous, delirious game. This dimension is given a higher status than the others. Consequently, according to Caillois' typology, we have a one-dimensional development of one category. We have to have a combination of all four dimensions in order to produce a really comprehensive game.

TL *You say somewhere that when desire has been satisfied, people experience a kind of mental death. To what extent is this an exaggeration, and how do you understand the rhetorical function embedded in your style of writing?*

I am very aware of the paradoxical rhetoric in my writing, a rhetoric that exceeds its own probability. The terms are purposefully exaggerated. If truth does not exist, then we have to proceed behind the metaphysical scenario of subjects and objects. I like to explore in my writing what happens after the demise of different things and truths, and this can only be done through the use of thought experiments. Of course this is not a discourse on truth – not everything can be verified, there is no pretence about that. The same goes for the question of desire. To say that all desires are satisfied is nonsensical because desire as such cannot be satisfied, quite the opposite. But in this world of production, desire is at one and the same time both productive and a means of satisfaction. Consequently we have lost touch with the whole concept of desire: desire as metaphor, desire as promise, as something that cannot be satisfied or made a reality. I don't use the term 'desire' very often. The term had its day in the 1960s and 1970s. I suppose it's the same for me with the term 'symbolic'. Many of these paradigmatic terms were coined for other eras. 'Desire' still clings to the world of the subject. Even Deleuze thinks of desire within a sphere of production, albeit a different and higher type of production. Molecular production was a big step for Deleuze, but even this proliferation and fractalisation of the term 'desire' kept its original form and was never developed further. I like to explore in my writing what happens when something ends.

POSTMODERN?

TL *How do you perceive 'postmodernism'?*

I have nothing to do with it. I don't know who came up with this term. It comes from architecture, doesn't it? I never understood why I was supposed to be a postmodernist. But when it comes to the book *Simulacres et simulation*, why not? It does not deal with a modernity that has a progressive finality or a technological development with clear boundaries that depicts an aftermath where nothing happens. We have always had simulation and simulacra, and perhaps also another level of virtuality. But I have no faith in 'postmodernism' as an analytical term. When people say: 'You are a postmodernist', I answer: 'Well, why not?' The term simply avoids the issue itself.

TL *Could the term 'transmodernism' better describe our time?*

This is a far more interesting term. I am not the only one to use it. For example, Paul Virilio uses the term 'transpolitical'. The term analyses how things develop after the principles of political realism have disappeared. When this happens, we have a dimension where politics always has and always will exist, but it is not the real political game. What happens afterwards calls into play the same problematic, but is specifically connected to defined areas; we have transaesthetics, transeconomy, and so on. These are better terms than 'postmodernism'. It is not about modernity; it is about every system that has developed its mode of expression to the extent that it surpasses itself and its own logic. This is what I am trying to analyse.

TL *Nevertheless, the age we live in has its labels or defining characteristics. You have written that the epochal characteristic of the romantic era was replaced by surrealism, which was in turn superseded by transparency. You describe transparency as a nihilistic situation. What kind of nihilism are we talking about here?*

I'm not talking about transparency in the sense that you see everything on television, but that television is watching *you*. It is all about reversibility, in the worst sense. It is about visibility, the total disappearance of secrecy. Everything has to be visible, but not in a panoptical way where everything is visible to the naked eye. Transparency is more than just visibility – it is devoid of secrets. It is not just transparent to others, but also to the self. There is no longer any ontologically secret substance. I perceive this to be nihilism rather than postmodernism. To me, nihilism is a good thing – I am a nihilist, not a postmodernist.

For me, the question is precisely this: why is there nothing, rather than something? To search for nothing, nothingness or absence is a good type of nihilism, a Nietzschean, active nihilism, not a pessimistic nihilism.

SEDUCTION AND DEATH

TL *The director Ingmar Bergman once said that when he is dying, he does not want to be a vegetable in a hospital bed, but would like to control the process of his death, to avoid becoming a thing. You have written extensively about death. Have you formed any thoughts about your own death?*

I would say that it remains an issue very much connected to disappearing. There has to be an art of becoming visible as well as an art of disappearing. Disappearing cannot be a factual coincidence; it has to be an art. This can have several facets in writing or in drama. There may be an art to the biological aspects too, a seductive way of leaving the world. If it's a complete accident, it's a negative death.

TL *The French philosopher Michel Foucault died of AIDS. Was that a type of art of disappearing? What do you think about the way he disappeared and the legacy he left behind? Has he really disappeared as long as his work lives on?*

He clearly accepted the challenge of death. He knew the risks and made a choice. In a sense, this is another way of disappearing. He used the art of discretion, a safeguarding of confidentiality that was incredible – without in any way claiming that this is a good way to withdraw from the world! I would say that part of disappearing is to disappear before you die, to disappear before you have run dry, while you still have more to say. Many people and intellectuals are already dead but, unfortunately for them, continue to speak. This was not the case with Foucault.

23 The Antidote to the Global Lies in the Singular

Interview with Jean-François Paillard (J-F.P)

J-F.P *How does one become a major French intellectual?*

My career's been an atypical one. With grandparents who were peasant farmers in the Ardennes and parents who had moved to the town and become white-collar workers, I'm a member of that generation in which the sons of the middle classes were able to get into higher education without much difficulty. But I gave up on the idea of a prestigious teaching career early on. I was a secondary school teacher for a long time, but all I ever had to my name was the CAPES.[1] I didn't go to the École normale supérieure, which was the obligatory route into university teaching at the time. I didn't do a state doctorate either, and I never reached the rank of university professor, despite twenty years spent teaching sociology at the University of Nanterre at the invitation of Henri Lefebvre. Moreover, my first theoretical work came late in life: I was already 39 when *The System of Objects* was published in 1968. For a long time I was, admittedly, concerned more with political action than with writing . . .

J-F.P *That first work made something of a radical critique of the consumer society . . .*

More an analysis of the consumer object than a critique of the system as a whole. That would come a few years later with *The Consumer Society*, published in 1970.[2] The initial idea was to show how objects were both part of a social practice and a mythology, the act of purchasing being something both deeply material and highly symbolic. In fact there was a kind of misunderstanding from the beginning. My book dealt almost exclusively with the manufactured object. It explored its simultaneously physical and metaphysical dimensions. Coming at these two facets of the object was a way of beginning a dialogue with Marxism and psychoanalysis, which, between them, occupied most of the intellectual horizon at the time. Yet what people immediately took from this analysis was the famous critique of the consumer society . . .

J-F.P *And not without reason. As early as* The System of Objects,[3] *you write: 'In the current order, objects are not intended to be possessed but simply to be bought.' You try to lay down 'the rights and duties of the consumer'. You speak of the 'Father Christmas logic' of advertising . . .*

For thirty years now, as soon as a country has achieved a level of mass consumption, it has seized on *The System of Objects* and *The Consumer Society* and translated them into its own language. So these two works have never been out of print. For me, all the same, the books are part of a previous life and my work has gone in another direction . . . The concept of 'consumer society', like that of the 'society of the spectacle' which Guy Debord coined in 1967, has passed entirely into people's lives. They've been popularised to such a degree that they're really hackneyed now. You even find them in political discourse, which shows how far things have gone . . .

J-F.P *You went on then to attack the sacrosanct 'art object', which you saw simply as a commodity like any other . . .*

In the mid-1970s, the state created the Beaubourg Gallery (Centre Pompidou) and it became the mecca of 'culture for all'. This was the 'Beaubourg Effect'.[4] At the same time we saw an unprecedented, almost industrial, development of artistic works produced specifically for galleries, which came in the end to take themselves as their own subject. With one accord, artists set about borrowing the most banal of objects from reality and lumping them together – sometimes under cover of 'performances' – in installations that were of the order of scrapheaps, mere accumulations . . . I took the view that this approach was purely illustrative, that it ended in connivance – and ultimately collusion – with *things as they are*, and nothing more. Artists had, so to speak, become part of the wider game, had fallen into line. Nothing was being radically questioned any more – nothing whatever; no specifically artistic scene was being invented. All that was left was space-filling. An enormous accumulation of – banalised, commodified – 'art objects'. Like an enormous rekindling of Duchamp's stroke of genius that had raised the urinal to the status of work of art. Everything had become art and so nothing was art any more . . . At the same time, art, which was no longer reserved for the elite, became both an affair of state and an object of political strategy. That, too, was the 'Beaubourg effect'! It was an affair of state when – through sacralising the art object and the place where you commune with it – the aim was to cultivate 'the masses', that new 'silent majority', a vague, elusive entity that was beginning to appear with the first opinion polls and the books that were being written about it, such as Marshall McLuhan's. And it was an object of political strategy when it came to putting the masses to sleep, with the alibi of culture playing the role of safety valve and, ultimately, instrument of alienation.

J-F.P *Was that strategy successful in the end?*

I don't think so. The fact that the masses were thwarting that strategy on the part of power – through the media, among other means – had already struck me at the time. The masses are both alienated by political and media power and, at the same time, impose such a levelling-down of political and cultural discourse that they neutralise its impact, so to speak: everything foisted on them falls, as it were, into a great black hole, the hole of the indeterminate, the indecipherable. With the emergence of the masses, there's no comeback of political discourse; there isn't even any political representation any longer: there's nothing at all. As though the masses had become an object and were now taking their revenge on the world of objects.

J-F.P *Refusing, that being the case, to be manipulated . . .*

Manipulation, co-optation – I'm wary of these terms that presuppose an intention or some great organising instance, terms that assume a centre where there isn't one. We'd like to see the system we live in, this famous capitalist system, governed by some kind of ruler. In fact, it's the internal logic of the Western system, both respected by – and imposing itself on – everyone, that dominates the world. Take the art market, for example. It's the essentially economic logic of that market, further encouraged by its mediatisation, that explains the aesthetic banality of contemporary art objects. Only the insane idea that artists escape this implacable process remains, as though they enjoyed some special privilege. A contradiction that is a product of the simulacrum in these times of globalisation.

J-F.P *A globalisation which could be said, in your view, to be the highest stage of the consumer society?*

It's undeniable that the entire planet has come to be organised in value terms today – a phenomenon made possible by the advent of mass consumption, the media's hold on society and the generalised use of digital technologies. No sphere of human activity, private or collective, is spared. We're dealing with a total system, a kind of integral reality that foists itself on us as a universal order . . . Between the themes of the global and the universal, there is, in fact, a false affinity. Universality is things like human rights and democracy, whereas globalisation refers to another register – technologies, the market, information. It seems implacable, irreversible. And destructive: it kills off all other cultures by forcibly assimilating them. And, indeed, the dilution of the universal into the global can be seen as something alarming today – for example, in the exploitation of human rights as an element of political marketing. Consequently, the important question seems to be to identify what cannot be reduced to globalisation, what doesn't play along in this new undeclared world war . . .

J-F.P *You speak, in this connection, of a Fourth World War . . .*

Quite. The first two put an end to colonialist Europe and to Nazism. The third, which we euphemistically call the Cold War, though it was a very real one, sealed the fate of communism. Note that on each occasion we've moved towards a more all-encompassing world order, more towards one world. And this process has now virtually reached its end. Hence the widespread sense that we're dealing with an enormous unified system today, an integral reality, in which the enemy is everywhere and nowhere. This is what I have in mind when I speak of a Fourth World War: the war globalisation wages on itself. In a globalised system, face-to-face conflict is no longer possible; there's no declared enemy any more, no territory to conquer. The system's gone too far – to the point where it eventually breaks down and begins to consume itself by secreting a form of inner corruption. Not corruption in the moral sense, but something like a dismantling of the whole, terrorism being the violent metaphor for this tension that is irreducible to the system. As though it played the role of a virus which, in the end, might be said to affect everyone's imagination, adding a supplementary element of tension to the system, though this time a symbolic and virtual one.

J-F.P *Your interpretation of terrorism, which you refuse to see as an immoral act, is rather iconoclastic.*

Either we analyse terrorism as a sort of power of evil originating elsewhere – in the depths of Islam, for example – and explanation gives way to value judgement, or we look beyond good and evil. Terrorism then appears as an answering of evil with evil, something like the shadow cast by the system of domination – a hegemonic system which foists itself on everyone in the name of a democratic or universalist discourse entirely at odds with its own actions. Has it not been in the name of a war against terror – what English-speakers call 'deterrence' – that the Western powers have imposed a kind of security terror on themselves? That's why I say that terrorism, as a power that has seeped into the system, is perhaps winning the battle.

J-F.P *And the United States is losing?*

There is one world power which, by merrily riding roughshod over the universal values in whose name it speaks, has lost all legitimacy. Since it no longer has any precise enemies, it's creating some for itself, of varying degrees of virtuality: Afghanistan, Iraq and, of course, terrorism – a vague, elusive, but convenient concept, since it can be seen as the ultimate power of evil. The problem is that nowadays the evil is largely virtual. A good example of this is Iraq, where the weapons of mass destruction have, after all, never been found. The worst thing is that, by claiming to fight this evil, centres of infection get created all over the place: Afghanistan, Iraq, Indonesia, Turkey and so on. As though the system were always running further into trouble by seeking to escape it.

J-F.P *In that respect, do you think September 11th was predictable?*

No, it is by definition an unpredictable event. An incident that springs up in a system with too much forward planning – a system that's too programmatic – is necessarily unpredictable. But its occurrence is possible. In a context of globalisation, political history is sinking into a slough of tedium. Representation doesn't work any more, the gaps between rich and poor yawn ever wider. And then, from time to time there's an explosion, a dramatic event, an 'accident' as my friend Paul Virilio would say. He's actually talking about an accident that could be apocalyptic . . .

J-F.P *Do you believe that?*

That's not the way I am. I don't think the world will come to an end that way, though in reality we simply have no idea. But I don't think we're moving into a classical cycle of – social, cultural or economic – crises, crisis being, after all, part of progress. I believe more in a process of a catastrophic type where, as I said before, the system, in trying to solve its problems, rushes further and further into the mire. And does so in all fields . . . You can see this, for example, in the area of information. We're aware there's a problem here. Images and messages have proliferated to such an extent, become so undifferentiated and impossible to sort out, that they've ended up preventing any form of exchange. Yet the proposed solutions to this problem merely generate even more images and messages. We are, then, in the presence of a catastrophic process . . . Still, there's something entertaining in the spectacle of the present world racing out of control and ultimately unhinging *itself*, incapable as it is of escaping its own logic, as though it were caught in its own trap.

J-F.P *What about the individual? Do you think individuals can exercise agency in this 'unhinged' world?*

I think a form of vitality remains in every human being, something irreducible that resists, a singularity of a metaphysical order that goes even beyond political commitment – not that that commitment has been entirely eliminated. So we must look to the singular for the antidote to the global. I have to tell you, in fact, that if I weren't convinced that there's something in the human being that fights and resists, I'd quite simply have given up writing, since, in that case, writing would be just tilting at windmills. I'm firmly of the belief that this particular, irreducible element can't be universalised or globalised, that it can't be part of some standard form of exchange. Will human beings do something positive with it one day? We can't say. The issue's by no means decided. And that, in fact, is where I find scope for optimism . . .

Translated by Chris Turner

NOTES

1. The CAPES – at the time, the acronym stood for *Certificat d'aptitude au professorat de l'enseignement secondaire* – is the major professional qualification for teaching in secondary schools and at the lower levels of the university system.

Students at the École normale supérieure wishing to teach in the higher reaches of the university system would normally take the competitive examination known as *l'Agrégation*.

2. J. Baudrillard (1998), *The Consumer Society: Myths and Structures*, London: Sage.
3. J. Baudrillard (1996), *The System of Objects*, London: Verso.
4. Baudrillard published the short text, *L'effet Beaubourg: Implosion et dissuasion* (Paris: Galilée) in 1977.

© 'The Antidote to the Global Lies in the Singular: An Interview with Jean Baudrillard', *Cultural Politics* 7(3), November 2011, 339–44.

Select Interviews and Dialogues

Baudrillard, J. (1998), *Paroxysm: Interviews with Philippe Petit*, London: Verso.

Baudrillard, J. (1999), *Le complot de l'art et Entrevues à propos du 'Complot de l'art'*, Paris: Sens et Tonka.

Baudrillard, J. and J. Nouvel (2002), *The Singular Objects of Architecture*, Minneapolis: University of Minnesota Press.

Baudrillard, J. (2004), *Fragments: Conversations with François L'Yvonnet*, London: Routledge.

Baudrillard, J. (2005), *The Conspiracy of Art: Manifestos, Texts, Interviews*, ed. S. Lotringer, New York: Semiotext(e)/MIT.

Baudrillard, J. (2014), *Les grands entretiens d'artpress*, Paris: imec éditeur/artpress.

Baudrillard, J. and M. Guillaume (2008), *Radical Alterity*, Los Angeles: Semiotext(e).

Baudrillard, J. with E. V. Noailles (2007), *Exiles from Dialogue*, Cambridge: Polity.

Gane, M. (ed.) (1993), *Baudrillard Live: Selected Interviews*, London: Routledge.

Books by Jean Baudrillard in English

The following list of books by Jean Baudrillard available in the English language is arranged, where applicable, in order of appearance in the original French. The first date indicates the publication of the English translation, the second, in square brackets, refers to the original French publication date. This list is expedient, containing books that are not solely by Baudrillard and some that are English-language publications in the first instance.

Baudrillard, J. (1996 [1968]), *The System of Objects* [trans. J. Benedict], London: Verso.

Baudrillard, J. (1998 [1970]), *The Consumer Society: Myths and Structures* [trans. C. Turner], London: Sage.

Baudrillard, J. (1981 [1972]), *For a Critique of the Political Economy of the Sign* [trans. C. Levin], St Louis: Telos.

Baudrillard, J. (1975 [1973]), *The Mirror of Production* [trans. M. Poster], St Louis: Telos.

Baudrillard, J. (1993 [1976]), *Symbolic Exchange and Death* [trans. I. H. Grant], London: Sage.

Baudrillard, J. (1987 [1977]), *Forget Foucault: Forget Baudrillard* [trans. P. Beitchman, N. Dufresne, L. Hildreth and M. Polizzotti], New York: Semiotext(e).

Baudrillard, J. (1983 [1978]), *In the Shadow of the Silent Majorities or The End of the Social and Other Essays* [trans. P. Foss, P. Patton and J. Johnston], New York: Semiotext(e).

Baudrillard, J. (2001 [1978]), *Stucco Angel* [trans. J. Hirschman], San Francisco: Deliriodendron Press.

Baudrillard, J. (1990 [1979]), *Seduction* [trans. B. Singer], London: Macmillan.

Baudrillard, J. (1994 [1981]), *Simulacra and Simulation* [trans. S. F. Glaser], Ann Arbor: University of Michigan Press.

Calle, S. and J. Baudrillard (1988 [1983]), *Suite vénitienne/Please Follow Me* [trans. D. Barash and D. Hatfield], Seattle: Bay Press.

Baudrillard, J. (1990 [1983]), *Fatal Strategies* [trans. P. Bietchman and W. G. J. Niesluchowski], London: Pluto.

Baudrillard, J. (2014 [1985]), *The Divine Left: A Chronicle of the Years 1977–1984* [trans. D. L. Sweet], Los Angeles: Semiotext(e).

Baudrillard, J. (1988 [1986]), *America* [trans. C. Turner], London: Verso.

Baudrillard, J. (1987 [1987]), *The Evil Demon of Images* [trans. P. Patton and P. Foss], Sydney: Power Institute Publications.

Baudrillard, J. (1988 [1987]), *The Ecstasy of Communication* [trans. B. Schutze and C. Schutze], New York: Semiotext(e).
Baudrillard, J. (1990 [1987]), *Cool Memories* [trans. C. Turner], London: Verso.
Baudrillard, J. (1990) *Revenge of the Crystal: Selected Writings on the Modern Object and its Destiny, 1968–1983* [trans. P. Foss and J. Pefanis], Sydney: Power Institute.
Baudrillard, J. (1993 [1990]), *The Transparency of Evil: Essays on Extreme Phenomena* [Trans J. Benedict], London: Verso.
Baudrillard, J. (1996 [1990]), *Cool Memories II, 1987–90* [trans. C. Turner], Cambridge: Polity.
Baudrillard, J. (1995 [1991]), *The Gulf War Did Not Take Place* [trans. P. Patton], Sydney: Power Publications.
Baudrillard, J. (1994 [1992]), *The Illusion of the End* [trans. C. Turner], Cambridge: Polity.
Gane, M. (1993), *Baudrillard Live: Selected Interviews*, London: Routledge.
Baudrillard, J. and M. Guillaume (2008 [1994/1998]), *Radical Alterity* [trans. A. Hodges], New York: Semiotext(e).
Baudrillard, J. (1996 [1995]), *The Perfect Crime* [trans. C. Turner], London: Verso.
Baudrillard, J. (1997 [1995]), *Fragments, Cool Memories III, 1991–1995* [trans. C. Turner], London: Verso.
Baudrillard, J. (1997) *Art and Artefact*, ed. N. Zurbrugg, London: Sage.
Baudrillard, J. (1998 [1997]), *Paroxysm: Interviews with Philippe Petit* [trans. C. Turner], London: Verso.
Baudrillard, J. (1999 [1999]), *Photographies, 1985–1998*, Ostfildern-Ruit: Hatje-Cantz.
Baudrillard, J. and L. Delahaye (1999 [1999]), *L'Autre* [trans. C. Turner], London: Phaidon.
Baudrillard, J. (2001 [1999]), *Impossible Exchange* [trans. C. Turner], London: Verso.
Baudrillard, J. (2000) *The Vital Illusion*, New York: Columbia University Press.
Baudrillard, J. (2002 [2000]), *Screened Out* [trans. C. Turner], London: Verso.
Baudrillard, J. and J. Nouvel (2002 [2000]), *The Singular Objects of Architecture* [trans. R. Bononno], Minneapolis: University of Minnesota Press.
Baudrillard, J. (2003 [2000]), *Cool Memories IV, 1995–2000* [trans. C. Turner], London: Verso.
Baudrillard, J. (2003 [2000]), *Passwords* [trans. C. Turner], London: Verso.
Baudrillard, J. (2001) *The Uncollected Baudrillard*, ed. G. Genosko, London: Sage.
Baudrillard, J. (2004 [2001]), *Fragments: Conversations with François L'Yvonnet* [trans. C. Turner], London: Routledge.
Baudrillard, J. (2011 [2001]), *Telemorphosis* [trans. D. S. Burk], Minneapolis: Univocal.
Baudrillard, J. (2002 [2002]), *The Spirit of Terrorism and Requiem for the Twin Towers* [trans. C. Turner], London: Verso.
Baudrillard, J. (2005 [2004]), *The Intelligence of Evil or The Lucidity Pact* [trans. C. Turner], London: Berg.
Baudrillard, J. (2005) *The Conspiracy of Art: Manifestos, Texts, Interviews*, ed. S. Lotringer, New York: Semiotext(e)/MIT.
Baudrillard, J. (2006 [2005]), *Cool Memories V (2000–2005)* [trans. C. Turner], Cambridge: Polity.
Baudrillard, J. with E. V. Noailles (2007 [2005]), *Exiles from Dialogue* [trans. C. Turner], Cambridge: Polity.
Baudrillard, J. (2006) *Utopia Deferred: Writings from* Utopie *(1967–1978)* [trans. S. Kendall], New York: Semiotext(e).

Baudrillard, J. (2009 [2007]), *Why Hasn't Everything Already Disappeared?* [trans. C. Turner], London: Seagull.
Baudrillard, J. (2010 [2008]), *Carnival and Cannibal, or the play of Global Antagonism* [trans. C. Turner], London: Seagull.
Baudrillard, J. (2010) *The Agony of Power* [trans. A. Hodges], Los Angeles: Semiotext(e).

Name Index

Subject Index